In A Sound World

T0054222

In A Sound World

Victor Segalen

Translated by Marie Roux and R.W.M. Hunt
With an essay by David Toop

In A Sound World

Victor Segalen

First published by Strange Attractor Press in 2021

Translation © R.W.M. Hunt & Marie Roux
Essay © David Toop

Image on vi © Bibliothèque nationale de France, département
Estampes et photographie.

ISBN: 9781907222801

Distributed by The MIT Press, Cambridge, Massachusetts.
And London, England.

Printed and bound in Estonia by Tallinna Raamatutrükikoda

Strange Attractor Press
BM SAP, London, WC1N 3XX UK
www.strangeattractor.co.uk

Contents

Galloping Rhythm Will Traverse Him

An Introduction to Victor Segalen's Sensorial, Internal and Geographical Explorations

The idea for this series of translations came about some time ago. After inquiring about a French book that I had read and hoped to share with people in English, yet, for which there didn't appear to be a translation available, I considered that making the translation myself could be a potentially interesting endeavour. But whilst discussing the possibility of the project with the writer and musician David Toop, I was made aware of another book that he had long wished be made available in English, Victor Segalen's *Dans un Monde Sonore*, or, *In a Sound World*. This, I thought, was a more realistic undertaking. It also seemed to fulfil an original and curious purpose; a strange work of fiction, originally published in 1907, that located the experience of sound at the centre of its curious plot.

It is a story that has remained discordant and opaque to us as translators even as we have worked intimately with it, the peculiarities becoming most evident while in the act of attempting to describe its themes and machinations in conversation. We had to constantly re-imagine a delicate topography of sound, resonances, echoes and voices; sonorous evocations that loop back and forth between two languages in order to help us re-write Segalen's idiosyncratically long sentences and ellipses—and the personal internal thoughts of the story's narrator, Mr Leurais, as he makes his first steps into this acoustic world.

We made field trips to echoing caves and re-read poetry that appeared to reverberate appropriately against certain moments of Segalen's writings, finding points of resonant inspiration in varied literary precedents (ranging from Paul Valéry with his poem *Orpheus*, to Mallarmé's *L'apres-midi d'un Faune*, and Baudelaire's *The Voyage* to Aleister Crowley's *Mathilde*).

In our quotidian perceptions, we place so much faith in our ability to orientate ourselves within the visual world. As a result, we feel an acute sense of loss, dislocation and bewilderment when we may be required to rely primarily upon our auditory sense. Yet, perversely, such encounters also carry their own sense of expansion and exhilaration.

We discovered that among his many works Segalen had also written an essay entitled 'Synaesthetics and the Symbolist School', and a libretto for the composer Claude Debussy. Seeing thematic correlations between these and this volume's title story, we continued the translation process into these texts and have made them available to readers of English for the first time. They add some conceptual colour to the title story, and in some ways extend its original concerns: the essay might be read as a theoretical companion to it, while the libretto provides Segalen's personal interpretation of the myth of Orpheus.

In a Sound World forms a semi-trilogy with *Voix Mortes* and *Les Immémoriaux* (both 1907), all signed by the pseudonymous Max-Anély. In these works Segalen wrote about witnessing what he felt to be disappearing from the world around him; about conceptions of purity and difference. One possible reason for so many of his writings remaining unpublished during his lifetime is how much of it he spent far from his native France, travelling firstly through Polynesia and then China, where he witnessed and reflected upon the end of the Chinese empire while his own country experienced a pronounced flourishing of literary and artistic movements.

Segalen was by nature a frail being. As a sufferer of myopia, his mother had wished him to become a priest. Instead, he appeared to follow his own far-sighted ambitions, both lyrically and geographically. He developed a strong sense of spirituality that did not belong to the armatures of religion, but in his personal connections with places, involving both a reliance on scientific inquiry, fellow travellers, and explorations of oral cultures wherein the fantastic has a much more immediate relation to the real.

Before his first excursion as a military doctor in 1902, he met Saint-Pol-Roux, a Symbolist poet and intellectual who told him stories about Paul Gauguin. Coincidentally, his ship was given the mission to stop off in the French

Polynesian island of Nuku-Hiva and retrieve the late painter's belongings. Segalen acquired a couple of wood engravings to bring back to Saint-Pol-Roux and had access to a trunk containing Gauguin's late writings. An anecdote claims that, upon his arrival, he encountered a small oil painting which somehow came to be displayed upside down under the title of *Niagara Falls* by auctioneers in Papeete where Segalen bought it for a pittance. He assumed it to be Gauguin's "final canvas, completed in agony", which, in fact, "by a nostalgic paradox in this country of odorous clarity, portrayed a frigid Breton village beneath the snow." It was, allegedly, this disjunctive experience that served him as an allegory for his interpretations of Gauguin's life in Polynesia and that would inspire his own meditations on exoticism as an aesthetic of the diverse. From this followed an ongoing series of reflections borne from encounters with different cultures, which would become more profound later on, when he decided to travel further, constructing his own expeditions and research on Chinese culture.

He had studied the travel journals of such explorers as William Ellis and James Cook (who he called "the Quick Observer") and noticed the absence of anthropological survey or importance accorded to oral tradition. As a result, he would elaborate in the *Sound World* trilogy, through very varied forms of writing, his ideas on the damaging impact of colonialism and proselytism, collecting his sentiments of being in foreign places and developing his sensitivities to the violence of imperialism. In *Voix Mortes* he writes:

Voices have sung for perhaps, a thousand years, over thousands of islands without there being a trace to which paths they might have flown, or how they came to swathe such an enormous territory. The voices of the Polynesian Maori spread throughout the Pacific, they were sisters by language, by contour of melody, rhythm and finally, by race. [...] Cometh the white man and all is corrupted, falsified. [...] Those who remain, speak only by denying their past [...] guided by liturgical chants derived from the overbearing Lutheran chorus: There was no revolt; free rhythm can be brought into order. [...] What will happen in the chaos to the auditory state which so acutely listens and reproduces the sound, the syllables and flittering chants as cannot be simply repeated?

[...] The [European] spectator, or listener, [...] perceivable by his sedentary and docile custom, appears to be a sort of artificial and constrained being. He lives in embarrassment and dissimilation, with a stiff and awkward posture. Aloof, he shall endure magical evocations; galloping rhythm will traverse him and yet, motionless, he shall not run with them; coruscating song will swallow him. He will not dance.[1]

When it comes to the subject of synaesthesia, Segalen's first connection was simply that he was a subject of it. He had a mild form of sensory association whereby he sensed a correlation between sound and colour. Although it is possible that many of us may be subject to very mild forms of synaesthesia, should we interrogate ourselves deeply enough, it remains a mysterious attribute. He was clearly interested in the expression and experience of it, and once again, how one can gain a deeper sense of self through being subjected to it. With this in mind, one might reconsider his description "of a country of odorous clarity", or his affirmation that scents which "radiate a rarefied atmosphere under the shock of electrodes do not need candles to be seen."[2]

This provided a poetical provocation that he was able to study in his essay in relation to Symbolist poetry, a genre that was being analysed at the time as a possible substitute for religion through its evocation of human sentiments and the deep unity between the spiritual and the natural.

Segalen also often made excursions into mythology. *In a Sound World* invokes Orpheus so that he almost becomes a hallucination, a figurative conceit to address our abstract relationship with sound.

He wrote *Orpheus Rex* as a libretto, the story of a human-turned-tragic hero who reveals himself through his ability to exist within the beauty of his harmonies. The elements around him are referred to as 'Myriad Voices'; they echo, they 'murmurate in Unison'. His interest is expressed in some notes written in the margin of an early draft: "Orpheus will not be as the Sun, he will not be harnessed to generate life, nor any aspect of life [...] but as a human who creates, an inventor, a descendant, a human struggling among others ..." And so exoticism makes way for a mythic Classicism of fictional places and distant times.

In a letter to his wife from 1909, Segalen writes "I needed some kind of trampoline from which I could then free myself like Maeterlinck and Orpheus."[3]

And thus, this circle of ideas remains unendingly sequential, unsettled and opaque. Translating and rereading again and again does not entirely divulge, amongst the sensitive world of movements, echoes, sonorities, instrumental voices, perditions and revelations, who Orpheus, André, Mathilde or Mr Leurais really are …

M.R.

Notes

1 'Hommage à Saint-Pol-Roux', in *Œuvres Complètes de Victor Segalen*, Paris, Robert Laffont, 1995.
2 *Voix Mortes: Musiques Maories*. Éditions Novetlé, 1995.
3 Translated from Segalen's letters from China - *Lettres de Chine*, Poche, 1993.

Image on p.vi: Recueil. Mission archéologique, Chine, 1914. Kiang-k'eou [Jiangkou]] : [lot de photographies] / [Victor Segalen, Augusto Gilbert de Voisins, Jean Lartigue]

In A Sound World

In A Sound World

I do not know now what caused me to revive the old acquaintance. It wasn't until after I had left Bordeaux that we'd fallen out of touch completely, but that journey through Malaysia had only extinguished a friendship which was already beginning to languish.

His colleagues in the physics department seemed reserved in their account of his situation, and what I heard from the two faculty attendants left me disquieted: He lived out there, with little income, in a villa on the outskirts of the Benauge district, rustling among a few vine groves—and from there, he ventured no more.

Despite this, his wife was said to have remained implacably devoted. She was pitied in her isolation which was felt to be little more than a fruitless obligation. There were whispers; there was silence. All this I learned upon my return—I was very curious, and in a flash I felt my sympathy for this old comrade revivify; I also imagined what the grip of seclusion might have made of Mathilde, whose passionate nature I knew; though, she had never become my mistress.

To tell the truth, the thing might at once seem obvious, and complicated, for her husband had shown me a demonstrative affection. On the other hand, the occasion, the spark, the pretext had always been wanting. Thus, I presented myself at their home with little reason for remorse in the past, but resolved to provide abundantly for it, hereafter.

At the door I greeted her with no great show of affection. For her part she did not emit that stifled sound—the sound the tragic emit when reuniting; there was no profound silence. To my greeting she answered with a mere, "It is nice to see you," too frank, I felt, for there not to be some game afoot; it left me uneasy.

I ventured, "So how's André?"

"Bad. Terribly bad."

She went quiet. Her face was serious and straight. I shuddered. I avoid straight talk and am afraid of seriousness, especially since, out of prudence, I have consigned my life to the moment; direct reflections—a lip's poise, brooding shadows, brief gleams ... I looked at her.

She repeated: "Bad," and waited.

I understood that she expected a sign of encouragement and I entered, of my own accord, into a small drawing-room. I found it to be too low and too sunny; too brash to consider an amorous divulgence. Instead I ventured: "Is he suffering? The stress of his work, his lectures... in the pursuit of 'Science'? When I left he seemed so well; though ..."

"Physically? He has always been fit ... he has kept his appetite. But I fear he's become very;—very affected."

"His lungs? Or, has he a heart condition?"

I questioned with no purpose other than to speak in my turn, as is customary during embarrassed confessions. At the same time I noted offhand, how the allure of the pretty Mathilde of old was still smouldering and that two years of quiet home life had in no way diminished her charms.

The serene pleasure that this engendered allowed me, for a moment, to forget all the rest.—The rest? But I did not know anything yet ...

"First of all," implored Mathilde, "promise me you won't repeat this to anyone."

I promised. We always promise. There is no example of a friend who, solicited by mystery and taxed thereby to solemn discretion, has, in the first instance, rejected the onus. It is an amiable, intimate, and confident preamble, which so gently conceals our furtive betrayals. I promised.

"You are the only one I can resign myself to in admitting this. People around us do not suspect anything. For one thing we see no one now. Our old friends have largely neglected us. Those who might be concerned imagine him to be simply absorbed in his researches. I do not correct them."

I reiterated my pledge of silence in order to hasten the avowal. I even added:

"Count, my dear friend, that I am prepared to offer you any service."

"Nothing to be done. He is mad."

This was said very calmly. I felt more moved by that than by what any lamentation, confessed through waves of sobs, could imbue. At the same time, I imagined, behind Mathilde, the dislocated face of a furious man, clinging to iron bars, which he chewed at by twisting his neck. A mad man! I couldn't imagine it differently.

As if Mathilde guessed:

"But he is not dangerous ... Anyway, you'll see. Don't be surprised."

She passed before me.

***

We climbed a staircase entirely covered with a spongy carpet, which swaddled our steps in austere silence: a precaution against 'his' falls, no doubt.

I tried to compose a suitable attitude: How does one approach a madman? By remaining impenetrable and stern in order to impose a sense of decorum? Or better, a jovial air; the flippant jester?

I had barely made my mind up when Mathilde opened a door: a continuous, soft, transparent sound sank into my ears.

My jester took flight; it was evidently in a state of astonishment that I took the hand held out to me, the simplest act in the world.

"You see! Monsieur Leurais does not forget his old comrades," joked Mathilde, undoubtedly to explain my unexpected entrance. I added: "I must apologise for myself, I do not know how many years have slipped away between us ..." And I began to take refuge in a deliberately convoluted excuse when I was stopped by the very sound of my own voice.

Was it the resonance peculiar to this room, both very large and very empty, though at the same time, cluttered with disparate objects; or else of my imagining ... I heard myself speak as though each syllable I uttered passed through a harmonising orchestra; and in the dim I was dazzled with surprise.

André took my hand in a gesture of warmth: "That brave Leurais has not changed, not changed one bit!" He said, turning his head away, leaving me astonished that there could be so much sympathy in his voice, while his gaze remained oblique and vacant.

"And what has become of you after all this time?"

Mechanically, we each sat down. I leapt on this opportunity for a diversion, recounting at leisure my travels and the ethnographical survey which I had decided to accompany as far as Murray Island in the Straits of Torres. For eight months we had collected sensory data from the indigenous Papuans.

So often had I repeated my tale—with as many anecdotes as the story would allow and, from time to time, a disturbing incident to keep the attention of the listeners— that the story largely unwound on its own.

I was left free to examine the situation I found myself in. I had become accustomed to the resonance of my words, I even took some pleasure in it: the pleasure one can have— I've had it—of singing in a train travelling at full steam; to feel the voice embolden and swell with the rumble of the continuous organ ...

I felt sanctioned to speak without the fear of causing impatience, without the presence of agitation. It seemed that André had grown old; I affirmed it on the faith of remote memories, but I could not be sure—My view was obscure, I saw him only in profile, sitting at his desk, partially hidden by a clutter of instruments.

I was drawing to my conclusions on the expedition's findings (that I believe the senses of uncivilised people do not differ in primal acuity from the senses of refined societies— that the savage owes his sharp sight only to a more skilful interpretation of the familiar objects which surround him, and especially to his practical knowledge of distinct aspects: reefs along the coast, thickets upon a hillside) when my friend seemed to grow impatient.

With a brief glance I queried his wife; obviously, my words worried her too—undoubtedly for André's sake. I had forgotten myself. How now to proceed? For I was still ignorant of what form—what mania—my friend should be classified under.

One has no right to be mad as one sees fit, for even in the ravings of the supposedly discordant mind, adrift from the anchor of reason and free of the stays and stanchions of common sense, one must observe the rules and act within the prescribed diagnosis. Otherwise, in madness, one is declared an imposter. Now, André was not acting: Of this I was sure: One can hoodwink an expert, one cannot deceive a woman. And Mathilde, of course, knew what to expect from it. All this—passing in a whirlwind amid our mutual embarrassment—convinced me of my grave blunder. He will surely despatch me.

"We are keeping you for dinner, aren't we?"

His wife seized on this interruption to explain all the possible, simple ways I might return to Bordeaux that night and offered to fetch the local train timetable. I accepted. She left us.

My friend smiled sadly, and made a resigned gesture toward the door which she shut without any noise:

"Did you not notice anything?"

I followed his hand, then looked back at his face which he had not once presented clearly.

"No, I did not notice anything."

"You remember what troubles my last lectures put me in with the University, and how I decided to resign suddenly … And what stage my installation is at, I think I wrote to you—you alone, by the way."

"Perfectly." I was ignorant of everything, but I did not want to deter him.

"You went to great length …" I coughed.

"Oh, nothing is yet completed or definitive. With the exception of this room where I almost entirely live out my days; everything is still to be done around the house … to be redone … because … I will come to that. But one cannot hear oneself like this!" He grimaced and rose.

By a panel of levers he deftly began to turn handles arrayed above a copper pipe. Suddenly there was a crisp and disagreeable silence which interrupted the continuous drone that had not ceased since my arrival.

I felt it now to have receded from awareness as I had become accustomed to it until it had all but disappeared as one forgets everyday clarity. There was a sort of test whistle and then the song resumed, reinforced, blossomed, with further sets of harmonics and crackles …

André came back and sat down. In passing, he had drawn a drape and unmasked a whole shadowy panel:

"There!" he said with satisfaction.

—*There!* wheezed an indistinct sigh to which I turned my head—"Only the two of us ..." and then repeated, but from a most inhuman mouth. No, not a mouth ... exactly as the chatter of a crowd through a phone must sound. I stared at my friend in amazement. He did not perceive my confusion.

"I said to you then," he said;

—*I said* ... murmured the little voices.

" ... that as soon as my installation is finished, in my own time, in this house ..." The indefinite resonance prolonged each of its syllables and distracted me so that I missed almost all of his explanation.

I remember a few particularly descriptive phrases: "those backward crazy people ... that laboratory of ruminants who are rewarded with a lifetime of force-fed formulas to be forever re-digested."

Then, little by little, as my ears became adjusted to this bush of whispers, I began to follow. He concluded: "You understand, after all that, I had only one thing to do, to get away. But I did not hide my opinions. You would have done the same in my place?"

"Oh yes."

—Yes … continued the invisible chorus.

I coughed again, as if I had thought of clearing my voice or chasing with my ears those little buzzing echoes. The echoes coughed. Furtively, I looked at my friend in the vague expectation that he would at last perceive my stupor and, in a word, make it stop. But he stubbornly stalked onward into the void. And how can a maniac be questioned without fear of finding him, on a clumsy word, rushing toward you?

"Then," continued André, "I hoped for some rest. I was free, finished; the lessons that I had repeated indefinitely, from one year to the next, before an audience swollen with boredom, were over! I hurried back here—to my refuge."

Merely to show I was paying attention I interjected: "I wasn't aware you owned a house in the Benauge" but, mistrusting the inconceivable resonance, I spoke too quietly.

"What's that?" asked André.

"I didn't know; Ah!" … I cut off at random, widening in surprise.

André looked at me at last—no, not with his eyes …—but all his face, stretched towards me in what looked like a blind gesture, to wait for my words, which were somehow unworthy of this sudden attention. His ears flourished; more than is usual within the customs and attitudes of educated primates. Then he turned his head away. Again I was left with nothing more to consider than his motionless profile.

"This house came to me through my wife's uncle. However, in spite of myself, I am going to soon be parted of it: my poor Mathilde, I do not really know why, has a fear of it that she cannot get over."

"How come!?" I could not restrain my exclamation; so brutal, that the four walls sent it back as if it were a sonorous ball, and caused a copper cylinder close to a crystal vessel on the table to buzz.

"Your wife is sick, too?"

"I'll tell you, absolutely between us. My wife is ... but I can count on your confidence, eh? It is a thing which no one suspects!" These kinds of promises were becoming familiar to me:

"You can trust, my dear friend, that you have my full discretion; know, also, that I am disposed to you in any way that may be of service."

"Nothing to do: My wife is mad."

I smiled condescendingly; however, the idea of a demented Mathilde did not displease me at all, and I found a bitter pleasure in imagining the wild and abandoned aspect of this probable lover-to-be.

He continued: "I am surprised that it did not strike you earlier. It is true that ... That's why I interrupted you just now; clumsily! The story you were telling has parallels with our own, for it is precisely the mania which afflicts my wife.

"Understand that since we moved from the centre of Bordeaux—and it is to all those troubles which preceded that departure that I attribute her state today ... see for yourself: She is persuaded to live only through her eyes— they no longer conduct themselves calmly but flash off to the right, to the left, palpating, even, when by chance she merely finds herself in darkness!"

"But, that is a habit of mine as well," I ventured, "I confess that, although short-sighted, I endeavour to see as much as possible."

"Fool!" He added in a softer tone: "No. You want to convince me that the condition my wife bears hasn't the gravity which I attribute to it? Obviously, it's your role as a friend. But I, who have watched her for a long time and scrutinised even the least of her remarks, considering all that she has said, and guessed what she dared not tell me ... You do not know the distress that I have felt.

"Listen—for two years we had aligned our thoughts and feelings so intricately that we had intertwined the timbres of our voices ..."

He smiled with constraint, "would that not delight a poet? ... finally, consider this harmonious life and then suppose that one of these two beings, by some spiritual discord, detaches from the other, and gradually becomes indifferent, apathetic, alien, distant, and deaf ... deaf ... Ah! As if they each lived in a separate place ..." He confided: "My wife no longer lives for me in this world." He fell silent. I heard the echo of his last words faintly, and this echo seemed even more sad than his real voice.

With a certain refrain I uttered a banal phrase:

"One always exaggerates the illness of those whom one loves."

I was about to abandon myself, to sympathise, when I remembered that, in a madman, pain is not to be taken into consideration, since their emotions are outside the experience, the conception of normal people. This holds especially when it is in regard to the lamentable and delightful feminine form, wherein the reasons for pain are so numerous that one may treat as a fool he who goes about forging new ones!

Decidedly then his madness was confirmed: His madness became mad;—who ever worried that a woman or a man should hesitate to walk about at night?

As for boasting of a mutual life in perennial harmony without shadows, without creases—Certainly it would be nice if it were so. But we must do without it; that is the natural state, is it not? Why should I pity my friend, in revolt against our "nature", or simply for being on the margins?

Instead I recollected the fine scent of Mathilde's hair, her eyes; and how with a few kisses I might be made to forget all these equivocal grievances.

"It was done," he continued, "in a manner so insidious, that it took me some time to register the early changes. She stupefied me by telling me that the light of day affects her enthusiasm, her joy of life … I giggled at her at first. Then I saw it. She really feared the darkness. But now I know why."

He assumed a mysterious air:

"She cannot hear in the dark."

"Eh?"

"She does not hear … That may not be very exact." Finally, "I cannot say it better …"

"Hmm."

"You wish to answer me, in a simple tone, that this is a burden with which one can live, and if not love one another with the old enthusiasm, at least tolerate without much resentment. Alas! no. This perversion of her as a sensorial being has upset everything with its affected manifestations. At first our tastes diverged, even the most insignificant of nuances. And these little discords are not, I assure you, negligible; she began to look everywhere for light, to rejoice crassly when it was sunny, to praise bright colours like a child, or … a savage."

I left him to his delirium and considered, in brief glances, every corner of the vibrating room. I tried to guess, in this enveloping murmur, the role of some shiny, dull, round, or stretched oddity, which lined the walls, drooped over rails or hung from the ceiling. Then I began to smile to myself: in the dull of the darkening day, I had discerned an enormous harp, against the wall, on my left; then another behind me, the latter half smothered under a felted curtain.

It was obviously rustling, as the numerous cylinders scattered over the furniture rustled;—I recognised them, belatedly, as resonators. As for those two bluish gleams that were flickering over there in their glass tubes. Ha ha! I held the source of my 'little voices': two singing flames, doubtless slightly discordant in order to overlay the sound with thrums and undulations; nothing more than this elementary acoustic tackle.

Of course! Was it not precisely on account of disagreements over his acoustic ramblings that my friend had suspended his lectures at the University ... and had he not fallen out with his colleagues over the very same subject? What was astonishing in anything I saw? It was merely his apparatus: hydrogen lamps ... sounding tables. I had not been able to see the wood for the trees; that now, with his mind lost, this had become his folly, his favourite game. It was all simply commonplace; I was naturally disappointed. He continued to speak of her.

"You see, my wife has regressed in a short time to the state of mind of a ten-year-old child, or a savage from some Australia, or, still worse. Now this is a wholly subjective and painfully personal idea. Imagine a soul from prehistory—I say 'soul' for simplification, and do not intend to speak in parables—a soul that once inhabited a primitively feminine body, at a time when eyes were keened for the sight of prey which the hands strangled and tore through; now imagine that this soul has returned to impose itself and merge into the body of one of our contemporary sisters, and to stifle in her the possibility of all the feelings that we have acquired over the course of thousands of generations.

"So, this being—erratic; not errant, see?—erratic, that's it, and awkward, and confused; no longer could she hear like us, divine like us, resound to our triumphs; she could lead only a pitiful existence compared to such a being ..." He fell silent. Then he repeated more slowly: "...To such a being who unfortunately has preserved his presence of mind to savour sound; to contemplate with wonder all the harmony of this world of ours, the only one that is intelligible and enchanting to us.

"I tell you, the strange mental state that has afflicted my wife and the grief that weighs on our duality are beyond daily expression. I had said at first: hysteria, and by it I was saddened; I later confessed: Madness, and I wept; but, perhaps you feel it yourself, there is, in our discord, something other than all that, and which terrifies me."

The logic of these last words left me astounded. Obviously I was dealing with a madman. It was unquestionable. To be sure of it, I obstinately repeated to myself 'madness, madness.' In spite of everything, this vision of a manic husband watching an imaginary insanity take hold of his wife was a spectacle full of sad irony. I would prefer agitated ramifications, laden with absurdity, for example: 'I am the great Lama of Tibet.' That's how to talk crazy.

Thus, one would gauge it, judge it immediately, one would know what to rely on. The words of my friend disquieted me for their appearance of reason. And I mistrusted, with resentment, the degree to which the stories converged in this way with the sense of a 'normal man' that each of us is granted to assert of himself.

From then on, I listened to him more intently. He continued:

"After the exasperation of her sight, there was the obtusion of her auditory sense ... No, not even that. She is not deaf. I should prefer that so much! But, there is manifested within her a perversion of hearing which makes her neglect the most elementary awareness of everyday life and find sanctuary in the environment and habits of a primitive and base creature ... You cannot imagine the amazing way in which she has furnished the entire living area, almost the whole house ..."

I confessed that the drawing-room had seemed to me a touch garish in its raw clarity.

"Is it not? Is it not!" warming to my answer, "Well! I had to tolerate those fantasies which confirm it to be a mania. I take refuge in this room where I've settled in a less extravagant fashion ..."

"Ah?"

"Only in order not to contradict her too much, did I permit for the window I had walled up to be reopened. My poor wife 'cannot live,' she told me, in an apartment without light."

"Indeed," I ventured ambiguously. He was delusioned.

"Yes, it's very strange. But all the fantasies of the sun are nothing compared with her aberrations in the order of touch—within the realm of civilised movement she makes the most vulgar gestures. This is where what has become of her shows itself naked. And it's frightful; introduce an unusual object and she will seize it in both hands, shiver, sigh ... almost;—she will even sniff at it! One suddenly feels, a very imminent return of our antediluvian past—when the deaf men again, among the harmonious world, stood to conduct themselves, to live, by the vilest sensations ... when they thought they knew everything, fixed everything and understood everything through their anthropoid eyes and their clumsy paws."

Certainly I had not noticed any of this for myself; but the proposition stirred in me an indisputable excitement. In order to relieve André and thus allow him to disclose further, I reminded him that a woman—who is so close in appearance to the one she loves—must remain, in reality, dissimilar and forever alien; so much so that she was considered to be the female of a different species, more refined and slimmer than our species of 'man,' the male of which had disappeared before our time, whilst we were also deserted, losing our own, broader companions to a similar extinction.

He exasperated himself:

"You talk to me like a pedant. You have understood nothing of what I am trying to explain; yet I've told you too much to stop here—I'm obliged to relay some adventures that are rather obscure ..."

I hoped so! And in that instant I forgot my conviction of obvious madness, and I voluntarily endeavoured to accept his propositions.

André rose again with a new and sudden impatience:

"Nothing works today!"

And he disappeared into a darker recess: two other little flames began to quiver, died back, reappeared. A twilight enveloped the room, preceding that of the day's own fall. I do not know why I murmured:

"No! Not yet ... no light yet ..."

André turned away.

"Eh! You too think I'm crazy?"

He then whipped up the flames which darted in pinkish tongues, whisked with blue, but cast no further light. Another simmering crystal sprang, hesitated, changed and resolved into an imperturbable song, which, reinforcing the first, splashed the walls, filtered through the strings and swelled them into sound. André pulled away all the drapes: an equivocal wave exhaled from all four walls.

It appeared to me that everything was clearing and that everything was illuminated—but I wisely dismissed these gleams of unreason, for it was night, almost night. I was sure that nothing could be seen through the window; but how could I be sure? And then, who was talking about seeing? Was it only me who felt it necessary?

Abruptly I ceased to exasperate myself within this unfounded vacuum and, resting my spiralling head back into the armchair, I submitted myself to be bathed by the curious effluvia, where the morning tones and the timbre of the young sun shone at the dawn of dawn. I no longer even listened to my friend. His voice dissolved into the rumours of space. His speech, which had become rhythmic and had slowed to a swell, imposed itself within my reverie, rocking me, overwhelming me ...—really, who had spoken of 'seeing?'

"She is distant," he said, "she is distant, and only gets farther away. She is lost and every day disappears a little quicker. Our harmonies have vanished. How to recall the poor fugitive? I readily imagine Orpheus, the singer of hymns, abandoning the world of a thousand lyres, and descending to the infernal caves—by which one can take to symbolise exactly the brute material world, mute and deaf; this is the most ignoble and truest of all Myths that man has configured.

"Armed and adorned with magical harmonies, Orpheus subdues matter, rocks, sand and mud; it breathes, it moves, it propagates, it dominates and passes as a precursor amidst the general herd of early humanity—those who see; those who touch; those who smell; those *who do not hear*.

"And then, after so many arduous labours, having reached Eurydice, he abandoned himself and proclaimed the most thundering hymn to voluptuous joy ..."

—*Voluptuous joy*, repeated, with great thrall, the four walls and the vault. The echoes permeated each other. The room shone.

I hesitate to risk this comparison—one would have said a hall of mirrors; multiplying, repeating and collapsing into hundreds of varying visions. And then everything subdued and ceased. The flames that were singing returned to their serene tierce again ... Yes, a major third—how could I have not discerned it earlier—Was that it?

"Orpheus had thought he had recovered and conquered everything. He forgot the inevitable defilement this brutal world exacts, this world where we stare, where we smell, palpitate, haggle in flesh, where we are bruised, tumbled and troubled. His love for Eurydice and his desire to love her still remained pure, free and harmonious. Even before he'd left the infernal vaults, not doubting the power of his lyre over the recovered divinity, he wanted to rejoice in love.

"—He sang ..."

—*Sang* ... resonated the room. But the blossoming third of the lamps undertook a disturbing concord: a tertiary note, very poignant and bitter, imposed its augmented fifth; ah, that dissonance! I never could feel it otherwise; a will loaded with anguish ...

"He sang! The astonished woman rolled her eyes in questioning gaze, then lowered them, then raised them, now full-gleaming, which Orpheus recognised to be immodest. She bent her knees and sat down among the dusky black hills, which took hold of her toes, her ankles, and climbed up her legs. Her outstretched arm slumped across the earth, and her wrists' blue flesh gradually sank. The uneducated singer, standing before her, spread over her his hymns as caresses and, through striving in song, exhausted himself.

"Through the rhythm of his words, through the bursts of the awakened chords, by all the quivering of his nuptial lyre, he brought his lover to the conjugated emotion of their double understanding.

"—She was waiting. Orpheus lavished more unusual kisses.

"She waited; And became impatient. Her hand, which had been kneading the mud, furrowed the hem of her veil, stroked the obscene curve of her belly and reached the brass loop through which her belt was tied; she begun to unknot it.

"Powerless, Orpheus was silent. There was an inexpressible silence in Hades. In abject disgust he contemplated this woman, once like the Apollonian zither, whose five passions corresponded to the five sonorous modes of love. She appeared metamorphosed by malevolence; nothing but the feminine thirst for primitive lust—where one shocks, one bites, one penetrates ... He stepped back to escape the defilement, and despised the unclean rite. With a loud voice he tore the weft of his lyre; the bent shell struck him in the chest, and the strings, snapping, bit his wrists and tore his nails. Eurydice, smiling, opened her tunic. Orpheus fled; he turned not."

* * *

The flames still sang. I do not know how much time passed. But who would have been worried about time? And why not demand from me the date? Only, I recall asking, at an indeterminate moment, and almost instinctively:

"Orpheus, is that ... you?" I was confounded.

"No," replied André, "Orpheus is not I. Orpheus was not a man, nor a being, living or dead.

"I can imagine how the allegory I have just offered you bursts against your classical recollections. I believe it to be true, however, to the exclusion of those teachings. Orpheus? It is, in our evolving humanity, the desire to hear and be heard; the power to live and create in sonority; it is the ideal symbol of our escape from the dank and crude score of our Archean sensations rendered through base visions, wrought from staring, kneading, groping ...

"There's no evidence any Orpheus ever was, as a being; only Orphic powers, whose apogee, in our present humanity, allows us to conceive of the world in this way: a sonic essence from which proceeds a whole series of attributes which once dominated; the extent of things, the movement! What one saw, what one touched! Ah! Oh! These puerilities! However, I will concede to you that in this evolution there may have been beings—sketches of how we are now—who, long ago, distinguished themselves from their compatriots and cleared the path.

"These beings—you could proclaim them to be 'Orphies' as we say 'Promethei' for those whose hands first burst forth with fire. Back then they deified these precursors, these deviants—inventors of broader sensations. Now we lock them up. Sometimes they are decorated.

"I might imagine myself as such an oracle. But for all that—a pedestal among the clouds, an honorary diploma; none of it would restore to me the one who disappears and is compelled ..."

"Your Eurydice?"

—*Eurydice* whistled through the taut harp strings in unison. "Your wife?"

I cautiously halted in front of a big question of conjugal ignominy. He had planned for my inquiry:

"I cannot tell you any more about *our* story."

"Ah!"

***

Uncertain hours passed; or did not pass. The vibrations of the harps, still traversed by the triple song of the flames, sparkled sufficiently to occupy all my thoughts.

However, there came to me an idea that appeared stupid by dint of being both natural and simple:

"You must have a sublime love for music?"

I heard André softly chuckle:

"I do not know what you call 'music.'"

I answered my question in an embarrassed tone, and mixed up all sorts of incoherent facts, the link of which was that a single article of the dictionary had them under the same definition. But it is sometimes resting to speak thus, through random associations constructed from a default engine. In this way I scrolled: Helmholtz's studies of resonators, Ptolemy's range, the lower sounds systematised by M. Riemann. André chuckled away throughout my discourse.

"You seem to me singularly depressed by your journey to the Torres Straits."

He strove to cover the reproach in his voice with a little humour:

"Instead of trying to put glasses on the noses of savages, you would have done better to take care of your own repose. Well, you're obviously joking. But you know very well that all the people you talk of, all your 'musicians,' as they used to be called, were merely deft jugglers, they jumped on the octaves as if they were on stilts but they never suspected that essence which infiltrates us, animates us, makes us exist, 'that enormous song of the planets' which Pythagoras has predicted, and for which we hold so much contempt!

"They have never ... yes! Someone has found ... someone. But we do not know yet."

My friend fell silent, with a long sigh. The room sighed.

—*Dah!*

I closed my eyes abruptly; an unbearable yellow gleam struck the walls; I grimaced with surprise; André must have extinguished his three flames, for all the resonance fell silent.

The door opened:

"My friends, let's have dinner," said Mathilde, who was carrying a lamp with a woozy glow. Her face displeased me under the rays of that foolish light and her voice sounded fragile, dry and musty.

"Above all, do not be surprised!" said André, "I've had to yield so much to her!" and he slipped away, his face dismayed.

***

Again, I was struck by the spongy nature of the staircase; then, mechanically, I narrowed my eyes and rubbed them, feeling a need to stretch, after the astonishing confidence, and to relax I did not know what aspect of myself ... my ears maybe?

But as soon as I took my place at table, I had to answer to both Mathilde, who, while watching André, spoke sharply in a naïve manner, and André, who obviously deplored such small talk. There was, between these two beings, the tension of one, wary of the other, and at the same time, a deep reciprocal observation.

My friend seemed very awkward. Several times, his hands threatened my glass or struck his plate, or the edge of the table. His wife was impatient. After a sudden gesture, I exclaimed:

"André, you've cut yourself!"

It took him some time to perceive it:

"He does not feel anything," Mathilde said.

He felt nothing! The dinner was over, before I was aware of it.

The vague idea of leaving, the return journey, this 'train to be taken,' brought me back to the feeling of passing hours; time measured with clocks ... and I looked to see how much had been swept away.

"I was going to remind you it was late," said Mathilde, "although we are sorry to let you go. But you will come back, as soon as your conference is over?"

Why did she insist? André was worried and nervous, in the vestibule he hurriedly held out his hand.

"I confess, my dear fellow, that all these lights leave me dazed." And he left us almost brutally.

"Well?" Mathilde smiled sadly and gave me a consoling expression. She held the little lamp with its yellow flame, the same which had so drastically affected André's confidence and illuminated his gaunt features. Her lips, now I saw them from close range, appeared cracked under the light; a corner of her throat looked grainy; unalluring to the eye. I made an imprecise gesture, from which she could take encouragement, sympathy, hope. But in truth it was, in spite of myself, a disdain for her flesh which in me rose. She, my mistress! I had imagined … I laughed inwardly, and my laughter seemed to strike me as it had in the astonishing lair of her husband. She held out her hand. The contact displeased me by definitively stifling that ghost of desire I'd held out for her. It was a brief, trivial farewell. I turned back. She smiled again. What ! I knew it: Eurydice, the Mantis with wrists full of mud … I ran away.

***

The night and the perfume of the vines calmed me. The road was very long. I felt myself still dizzy with half-real resonances, and walked, bent over myself.

At a detour, in front of a white fence, fairly similar to the others, but which I recognised however, among them, an idea suddenly fell like a stake into my brain: it seemed that I had tripped over an internal obstacle; instinctively, I flung my head back.

"Obviously," I said to myself, "she and he do not belong to the same kind of feeling ... obviously they each inhabit a different world ... they mesh, they alternate for each other, perhaps they do not penetrate; they do not get along."

I gave a furious blow of a cane to the wire which bordered the road to my right. It echoed along its length, and it pleased me to divine it in my ears.

"A different world ... Two worlds!" An indescribable anguish took hold of me: "which one is mine, the one where I live, where I come and go ... And then, which one is the true world?" But this did not make sense. I corrected: "Which is the truest ... or the least false; the better?"

Thus I accumulated little useless epithets, and unwrapped an idle questionnaire.—Another blow of the cane, and a new metallic whipcrack.

Nothing answered, nor did I answer myself. Naturally, I *should* have concluded the unreality of one of these worlds without further ado: The new, the unusual, the 'unheard'.

And I was expecting the ready, the logical, the lazy solution: André was crazy: his wife had told me ... Yet this was argued with a half-hearted insistence. Moreover, I knew that this was the least valid hypothesis to adopt. If I tried I would only have to abandon it. Did I not share that 'madness' for a moment?

And then, a hundred yards further, as a path turned away to my left, beneath a black willow, everything changed.

Dry and imperative notions sprang up, and formulas came to my lips:

"Construction of the external world ... External perception is a true hallucination ..."

I felt, at the professorial façade of these reminiscences, my dogmatic spirit resume. Hippolyte Taine said ... but here Taine did not say, not, at least, in this form: "The *mechanical* conception of the universe is only a naïve simulacrum." Where did that come from? and this: "The idea of the object, the idea of the body, the idea of matter derives from the visual and tactile sensations which have been illegitimately erected as an entity ..." Other data of the same kind began to dance into my memory, like a swarm, but these were less precise:

"What children we are to explain that the impressions of the eye, the skin and the muscles are elevated to the dignity of external and permanent laws, above all other sensations. Why select and prioritise in this way?

—We have unduly wrung matter from the perceptions

of vision and touch, but we can imagine other matters, with totally different qualities that are related to us through our ears ... We would then affirm: matter is noise, nothingness; Is Silence ..." who, but who could have proposed this last aphorism?

Suddenly, all this deliberation broke down onto a red blanket, and I saw in an imaginary vision—ten or twelve volumes bound in the same shade. At the same time, my memory, adroitly trained to locate, to identify, recited to me:

"Alfred Binet, *The Soul and The Body*, Flammarion, publisher ... Library of Scientific Philosophy ..."

I did not expect such detail. I was astounded!

This was a hypothesis, an essay, a game, a "challenge," said the author "for the pleasure of metaphysics ..." and it happened that I came into contact—no! Still I falsely use these words of tactility— ...into resonance with this new way of conceiving the world around us! I had heard a being living in this new world! And the theory, thrown down as a wager by the psychologist from the bottom of his laboratory or inkwell, was coming into existence.

Keenly, taking the form—though this is only a secondary effect—even of a tragic drama between two discordant sensibilities; and here it is further complicated by arousal and love!

A beautiful matter, this time no longer to be discussed, but to contemplate, live with, toil, and to also rejoice in, perhaps, later; this was well worth a deep study; to truly be put into practice. I will not tell my adventure to anyone.

I will design it for myself, as well as I can—three characters, a story without adultery—O joy, without adultery! Was it ever even there ? I was now so detached from those reveries that they struck me as of no more value than a mean and worthless gesture. No, I must never have thought of it …

And had I not always doubted that he was mad? I shamelessly congratulated myself on my intellectual acumen and good fortune. But a worry took hold of me: How to convince my dear reader, even in an unctuous and servile introduction, of the room my hero is confined in, stretched with string, furnished with copper balls, flames, all colourless and singing … while his wife nurses, encircles and circumvents him?

From the outset all sympathies will go to the woman, to the poor sweet woman.

And my role, in this! I will be the traitor who does not betray; the deceptive friend who does not deceive, the undecided, the fellow who disappoints the public if not the husband … It's a sorry situation! And to what ignorance might I confess, it's serious literature!

No! I will write nothing, I will tell no one. But, as soon as I am despatched from this infernal conference, I shall return here, to find my friend. I shall sympathise with him in his splendid isolation—I will confirm his subtle sonorities …

A train rolled in, the loud grating from the switching of the rails and the shrieking of the brakes brought me from my wandering lyricism. I had reached the station. The lamp light was repugnant to my state. I slept heavily in a wagon.

***

The conference went on interminably.

The upshot was a delegation created to overhaul the reform of scientific education. The commission appointed a subcommittee and I was made the secretary and charged with all the work. This required two trips and took up a year. I heard no news from André.

I dared not write. Would a letter cause disharmony, be taken as a blunder, or an insult on my part?

I desired so much to find him like he had been, strengthened in his fortress of the listening soul!

When finally I was free, I returned to Bordeaux, and rushed to their home. Mathilde appeared in the doorway. She welcomed me with an air of joyful triumph. This raised my curiosity.

"How's André?" I asked.

"André? See for yourself: Recovered, my friend, cured! It makes me so happy!"

André came out with a vigour to his movement and a vibrance in his voice.

"You find me in better form than on your last visit, hey, old man?"

"But, what happened with…"

"That room up there? It's nonsense … Talk no more to me about it, except as a sick man's malaise … Now what about you?"

—He had denied himself! His wife looked up at him with blissful and satisfied pride, a good wife reassured ...

I could have strangled the both of them.

Max-Anély

Orpheus Rex

Foreword

To deliver this drama—libretto, if it should be—without the following prologue to explain its *raison d'etre*, would be a gross injustice to the Maestro; an ingratitude not merely toward the musician but also to the friend, both of whom are the singular man, Claude Debussy, who has given rise to this unfolding lyric. Though he is now held in reverence, within his lifetime he remained discrete and defiantly disdainful of fawning blandishments—yet, the executor, left waiting to sign off these lines and present a spectacle founded upon a name, can neither hide nor vaunt the intimate constructs required for the double-task here undertaken. One must write and maintain parallel elaboration without pretending to a common work. A work is an accomplishment, unique, if it realises itself within an art form; complex, but harmonious, if two modes are served together. In an authentic collaboration between a musician and a poet, one has to reconcile and endure wholly the offerings of the other. But what remains shall carry only these mute words, the lonely words; because they are the words of the poet alone, left here without music.

Yet 11 years ago the poet wrote, in covert honour of the musician and within an acknowledged agreement, that "Orpheus was not a man, nor a being, living or dead. Orpheus: the desire to hear and be heard, the force within the world of sound ..."

The musician responded: "Orpheus? ... The one from Gluck represents anecdotal detail and bathetic lamentation. The 'sound world' is an unexplored domain; don't you think there is something new to be said of the myth?"

This is how the inspiration was engendered. Conversations followed, terse but not taciturn. We spoke deeper than the dialogue. The things that were not said were gestured at; thoughts that were muted set the silence deeper. We were looking for the incantation of the syllables. Without confounding either the tone of a vowel or the meter of an arpeggio—two very diverse arts—we pursued a form that could allow these duel harmonies to co-exist equitably; and how do they co-exist? The verbal contours sacrificed to the future hymn. The lyricism of the words—words already so equivocal—gave space to the lyricism of the lyre, the song.

Under the words, beings were formulated generating the storm of inhuman drama. Some characters emerged from the limbo. One could perceive passive figures. In the middle of them, a stranger, mortal as any; thus stood Orpheus Rex. Then, to accord with the ways of the world, there was set an imaginatively created arabesque; the construction of a certain physical sphere, built of mountains, woods and rivers, poised architecturally out of matter, overgilded with palaces, dug through with fissures ... It took more than two years—An unmeasurable time of only an internal rhythm.

One day, in a sonorous light, the conjure of which the poet still retains from the shimmer he heard:

> *... clear, triumphant in the inaccessible distance,*
> THE SINGING VOICE
> *alone, singular, savagely pulsating ...*

and the musician announced: "This will be my lyrical testimony". It was necessary for us to accept the word 'testimony', though in the deaf world, the unsinging world, it resounds into oblivion. Here, one can believe death to be usurped in the great, final gesture of Orpheus' assault, in raising the lyre above the combat. Death in life—which is not always fiction—has happened here through song. The Mænads, through their flaying of him, have riven the voice of Orpheus. The vestures of language imitate less an actor in full flow than the clothes about his limbs or the mask of the hero.

If the voice of Orpheus be lost what is left is the pre-auditory terroir (one dare not say echo) in the world of men. Orpheus fled from their killing. He is aided by the gathering resonance that men have emitted along his path, and so follows after the gentle canticle of Eurydice as before ecstasy. Her pride at having been followed, her naïve joy, her jealous puerility as a pure virgin sacrificed to the man—so she says!—such are the conceits of the Mænad priestess, filled with a lust she considers religious—this woman, in love with the yearning flesh, whose stresses, while exacerbated by music, do not need music to cadence themselves. See also the ambiguous character of the Old Zither-Player— pagan chanter, demi-singer, musical centaur, gifted with the knowledge of how to simply attend, to listen, yet without the capacity of hearing. This power is reserved only for the true Eurydice, and for a moment; an instant, death is evanesced.

What will be read in this book is not the Orphean text of a king Debussy would have celebrated. That other text lies buried in a grave—his grave. This one, 'in black and white', on plain paper, offers only the revision that renounces the essential drama that music could profess should it have the words. I have stifled the verbal orchestra with its thousand timbres, I cremate it on a pyre of kindling, both to the memory of the great, dead musician and to my friend.

This is why, in delivering this drama, I must set this dedication only to him—

The sole name
of
CLAUDE DEBUSSY

Orpheus Rex

Cast

ORPHEUS
EURYDICE
AN OLD ZITHER-PLAYER
A PRIEST
A WARRIOR
A MÆNAD PRIESTESS
A CROWD OF RUMOURS
THE MÆNADS OF FURY

Scenes

IN HEROIC THRACE

Prologue and First Act:

THE MOUNTAIN.

Second Act:

THE WOOD AND THE RIVER.

Third Act:

THE PORTICO AND THE SEA.

Fourth Act:

THE TEMPLE UNDER THE EARTH AND THE BURIAL CHASM.

Epilogue:

THE MOUNTAIN AMID AN AOLEAN REVERBERANCE.

I

The Mountain

All lights are out. Behind a closed curtain, one hears clearly, triumphant, from an inaccessible distance,
THE SINGING VOICE
alone, singular, savagely pulsating ...

One can discern around it the iridescent oration of a polyphonic
LYRE
which, as the SINGING VOICE *takes breath, repeats the contours of the words and gives no quarter to silence.*

(Prologue)

Curtain opens.

One sees, enveloped by vast zones of terrestrial night,
a tumultuous mass of rough boulders that run down
as far as our outstretched hands; a half-lit sky spears
and glimmers, flushing the treetops high on the ridge ...

But it is from further back, beyond what is visible, that
we apprehend this SINGING VOICE
Approaching in the foreground, stage left,
TWO MEN
dressed in animal skins, bare legged and heads
uncovered, trudging wearily.

They listen and mutter as the singing continues.

THE ONE (to be THE PRIEST): The voice seems to come from yet farther away.

THE OTHER (to be THE WARRIOR): So far; will we ever reach it?

THE ONE: Strewth!—it seems to recede at our every step.

THE OTHER: So this night has followed the arc of the two before it; lost along unknown tracks, stalking after a sound.

THE ONE: The skies are clearing over the ridge ...

THE OTHER: Finally, we might perceive ...

They head on toward the ravine and amidst the tangled

bushes beneath the glowing ridge.

Stopping to one side:

...This is just infernal; a voice calls to us, we pay heed and it scarpers again. The song lures us only to mock us!

THE OTHER: Can you understand what's being sung?

THE ONE: Come on, hurry.

THE OTHER: But I've had enough of this dour day, there's not the light to cast a shadow; only the rain falls on our sorry heads.

THE ONE: Come on! Look up there! Someone to guide us!

Visible in the clearing is an old man, tall, standing still on the ridge, his face turned toward the far side of the mountain, with a four stringed zither slung at his hip.

THE OTHER: Must be some vagabond busker, eh?

THE OLD MAN:
                           Without turning

              Hush!

THE ONE: With respect, O zitherman, of undoubted intricate melody ...

He trips, sending stones cascading down the mountain.

THE OLD MAN:
With authority

Quiet! Just listen.

One can hear again, alone and singular.
THE SINGING VOICE
Impatient the two walk on toward the old man.

THE ONE: Tell us only this ...

THE OTHER: Who is that singer of unceasing song?

THE ONE: What path do we take to reach him?

THE OLD MAN: No! No, do not approach him.

But as he says this the two climb to the crest of the ridge and, on looking in the same direction as the old man:

THE ONE &
THE OTHER: Ah! *Emitted loudly in astonishment*

THE OLD MAN: Do be quiet, lest he take to his heels.

THE OTHER: Who is this singing man?

THE OLD MAN: Why? What could I know of him! Only that he suddenly appeared in these valleys. For two moons past I have listened; I listen again.

THE ONE: I know this much: he is the one that we've been searching for ...

THE OTHER: But how can he be so tall? Is it a trick of the fog that makes him seem to be a giant? We mustn't let him out of our sights ...

THE ONE: He's young, a foreigner, he has hair of gilted bronze; by the breadth of his chest, he must be a great herder, as he would make a great leader. Take us, old man, we must meet him.

THE OLD MAN: Go up to him? Talk to him? He'll run from us, I tell you.

THE ONE: Not once he understands what we've come for.

THE OLD MAN: Why? Who are you?

THE ONE: Judge for yourself—

> *THE ONE & THE OTHER take off their pelts.*

THE OLD MAN: These are the ceremonial vestments of a priest, and you are armed for a military procession ... What is it you want with him?

THE WARRIOR: Take us.

THE OLD MAN: I daren't. Nor would I choose to. What if he fell silent? What if he should disappear? That he could be immortal; how do you know of the danger? Listen. Listen again. This is not a son of the deaf earth nor of the mute sky; neither hath e'er conceived of such a being ... Woe if he were silenced! For pity—let be that which balms me so that my infirmities rejoice: I do not want to live outside the vivid air of his voice.

THE WARRIOR: You can't stop us! Now lead on.

THE PRIEST: If you refuse, you will lose him anyway; look, he's absquatulated. Strode off into this dank fog that has so confounded us.

THE OLD MAN: Come!

He hurries into the bushes and descends into the ravine on the other side. One sees him bathed in light, struggling through the undergrowth.

THE WARRIOR: Be careful, why would you take us into this thicket?

THE PRIEST: The scree's unstable! I'm slipping!

THE OLD MAN: Haste ye!

THE WARRIOR: Over such a precipice?

THE OLD MAN: Follow me.

THE PRIEST: What an ordure to reach this man.

THE WARRIOR: Is there not a clear path to be taken?

THE OLD MAN: No; one must make his own way to him.

The three disappear.
They can be heard descending deeper, the sounds receding …

But triumphant again,
THE VOICE
resurgent.—The three men will hear it now in full flow.
A vibrant light invades the deep end of the valley until it's met with the dawn.
The heavy shades dissolve away, sloughed off, rent open, the foreground boulders dissipate and the space is widened.

ACT 1 (scene i)

One can see a corrie and standing amidst the echoes
THE SINGER
in full voice, that in harmony with the LYRE creates a radiant moment; a hymn.

Then the three men also appear, first THE PRIEST, *followed by* THE WARRIOR *and, at a distance,* THE OLD MAN *with the zither.*

THE PRIEST & THE WARRIOR:
Approaching intently.

King of Thrace and lord of a hundred warriors, hail!

Silence
The first Silence. A cruel day. A solar day.

THE PRIEST: We declare you King of Thrace.

THE WARRIOR: We here proclaim you ... *aside.*

The first man who
didn't quiver on
becoming a 'king'

THE PRIEST: He didn't understand.

THE WARRIOR: Is he deaf?

THE PRIEST: Tell me, young stranger of such resplendent voice, might you hear what we say—You are King, King of the Thracian people.

THE WARRIOR: And Lord of the Hundred Warriors.

THE PRIEST: We need only a sign of assent from your face to run before you, lead you to the tribes and cities that call out your name.

THE WARRIOR: So you will follow us.

> THE SINGER
> *Makes no move.*

THE PRIEST: Do you wish for others to beseech you? A cortège to lead you—of minstrels and dancers?

THE WARRIOR: Do you want for weapons? An armour of polished bronze?

THE PRIEST:
> *Pointing to the old man.*

> This one will carry your
> zither and play out your
> songs before you.

THE OLD MAN: Let him be; what has he done for you? He cares for none of this.

THE WARRIOR: Where does he come from?

THE PRIEST: What language does he speak?

THE WARRIOR: Would you tell us his name?

THE OLD MAN: You have listened to him and you want to know his name!

THE WARRIOR: Why does he not grant us an answer?

THE PRIEST: We are offering him the reign of a noble kingdom; all that lies between the sea and the mountains!

THE WARRIOR: He would rather sing for bears and jackals!

THE PRIEST: It is true that his tongue is not one known to any man.

THE WARRIOR: Doesn't matter. He should reply to us.

He threatens him.
THE SINGER
without emotion, turns away toward the foot of the mountain.

THE OLD MAN: He's going, I told you he would! Leave me, stop harrying him, say not another word. Oh singer of resplendent voice, singer of the unknown hymn, flee me not in silence. Hah, I'm out of breath trying to follow you, who I only live to listen to …

THE SINGER
continues on …

THE OLD MAN: Master! Consider this—my fingers are

shaking ... But the strings tighten and swell themselves by the last anaphora of your voice ...

> *And raising up his zither, the old man casts a desperate*
> *call to summon those last remaining echoes.*
> THE SINGER
> *stops and turns without guile.*

THE OLD MAN:
> *Approaches a little more confidently*

> Please answer this—
> Not for me, I ask of
> nothing, but for them:

Where do you come from, what language do you speak; they want to know your name. I beg you, bowed as I am by age before you, you of mysterious race. In reverence to the songs that will flow from you; I beg you; cast to those beasts what name you hold so they might feast ... For at your name they will run along, forever from you; Master, say your name.

THE SINGER: Orpheus.

> *The name flashes throughout the mountain.*
> *The singer disappears into the undergrowth.*

THE WARRIOR: What was that? What was his name?

THE OLD MAN: His name ... is Orpheus!

And the old man hurries after THE SINGER.

THE WARRIOR: Orpheus! Ha! No man before has ever been called Orpheus!

THE PRIEST: Orpheus Tenebrous ... Orpheus Obscure; Orpheus The Blind, perhaps ... No one before has ever dared name themself: Orpheus!

THE WARRIOR: Is it an auspicious name?

THE PRIEST:
> *With exaltation*

It is a most auspicious name! It's a sign. It's the vernacular of the Oracle. I behold the revelation. We had to join this man. Everything is aluminated. All will be accomplished. Listen to the Oracle. Now we can spread the word. Set the valley ringing. It was thus predicted:

"This one who will tame the mountain people, this one, the singer-of-the-night, he sees through all the ears and hears from every eye?" Is that not him? Surely it is him.

THE WARRIOR: I don't get it. How does he see with ears or hear with eyes? This is obscure as his name. We have been gulled. Better we go back.

THE PRIEST:

Recalling his Oracle

"The one who sees with all his ears! ..."

THE OLD MAN:

Reappears

You've chased him off. He's too far now. I even hear the whisper of his name die away ... It is the grave's mire that we are digging! The mountain is empty; its weight pours through my chest ...

THE WARRIOR: The old man aggrieves himself without good sense. We'll find him again, this singer of yours!

THE OLD MAN: You won't succeed. Never more will you ... Ah! Ah! Dear me! Eurydice! Daughter ... Eurydice!

The shout of a child responds to the old man.
And appears
EURYDICE
(Lively, savage and soft: Obedient and spontaneous,
dressed as befits the daughter of a vagabond singer.)

THE OLD MAN: My daughter, he has gone, they incited him and he fled. Run fast now, follow the echo of his steps. You will reach him, bring him back ...

He sets EURYDICE along the path of THE SINGER.

THE WARRIOR: Ha ha ha! He's unleashed his daughter to the pleasures of a fine-throated husband!

THE PRIEST: Let the girl bring him back. The Oracle is not mistaken.

THE WARRIOR: Such wavering! He sings, yet doesn't speak, he hears and yet seems to be deaf. One salutes him as a king and he runs away. It's not the bearing of a gallant lion. Never before have I come across a man like him!

THE PRIEST: It is he.

The curtain closes.

EURYDICE's race continues—through the mountains she chases … We hear … We hear the shaking of ferns; abrading of brambles; the stopping, the going astray, the starting again, finally reaching …

(scene ii)

The curtain opens on the secluded lair of

ORPHEUS:

Alone, lurking like an animal in the foliage, panting.

Away from man. Away from the noise of man. Fleeing, fleeing, flying, I call, I listen, I sing, I listen, I hear only from the rocks, the beasts.

Ho! But I hear the noise of man ... Their tumult and insults! They've tracked me to the deep end of my silence. I thought my den invisible, impregnable, yet here they come with their spluttering words, again! Must I go on, ever fleeing, fleeing ... ah? But I'm tired now, yearning, yearning for the call of the heart of another! Oh, enter a song who is not my own!

Hark, no ... This is more soft, the folding of moths, the dew shaking off, too stealthy for the step of a jackal. It glides, gentle ...

Bare foot, barely meeting the earth, this is no man, these are not my familiar animals; nor the races of the wind that tears through the brambles; something I don't know of is coming toward me.

What?!

Appears

EURYDICE

She stops, frozen. They stare; savagely, they consider each other. Eurydice murmurs:

Where did I come from? Why am I here? My father said ... He said ...

Oh! There's your lyre. How big she is, how poised! how tight her strings ...

She has so many—4, 8, 12 ... 12 strings, is that even allowed?

She comes closer.

Can I hold it?

ORPHEUS
rises and gestures.

EURYDICE: No? You wish me not to? Why? Is she heavy? I can play a bit on the tetrachord—My father, when his fingers become tired, he sends for me. I take up his song and play for our nobles. That was what he taught me for. But who taught you? What was your master called? I've heard said you can charm wild animals and set the stones to dance, they say it so throughout the villages, and...—Did you really fall from the sky?

ORPHEUS: Your voice ...

EURYDICE: You sing your words, but would you speak like they do?

ORPHEUS: Your voice ...

EURYDICE: You don't say this like the others, like men do. When I sing at their feasts and they've drunk a lot, they take me in their arms and swear that they love me ... No! I don't let them ... but they are swarthy and rough with their arms. You, your face, your knuckles are white. Have you no wish to live amongst men?

ORPHEUS
stands up agitated.

EURYDICE: The two strangers—why were they looking for you? They implored you to be their King.

ORPHEUS:
Hails the mountains in an imperial gesture and raises his lyre.

I am King.

EURYDICE:
Steps back with respect.

Oh you will live in a house with painted columns, you will dress in softly woven garments and hold the heavy twi-billed axe. You will hear the people repeating your words as the rivers murmur to the sea; the sea as it quells sometimes, wails sometimes, swells ... like nothing else ... And you will reign!

ORPHEUS: I am the King.

EURYDICE: And I shall be your servant.

ORPHEUS: But who has possessed you with the sound of your voice ...?

EURYDICE: I don't know; would it be you? For two moons past I have heard no other ... My father has followed, devoted in silence. My father! I forgot, my message for you—he grieves for the thought that you would depart. Come back for the sake of him who venerates you so.

She retreats.

Here lies your way ...

ORPHEUS: I love ...

EURYDICE: Come ...

ORPHEUS: Your voice ...

EURYDICE:
              Suddenly afraid—stops ...

   As the others do?

              Hesitant for a moment ...

   Yet, you don't force me to your arms.

ORPHEUS: Why?

EURYDICE: You do not try to grasp me to you?

ORPHEUS: Do you wish me to?

EURYDICE: I saw it well. You are not like other men.

ORPHEUS: I love ...

EURYDICE: Yes, and you haven't even hurt me yet.

She coyly offers him her hand, bringing him to her, directing him. They walk back toward the ridge of the mountains, the rumours, the men.
The curtain falls at the moment he reaches her.

II

The Wood And The River

ACT II (scene i)

The curtain opens.
In the foreground, among
the trees of a gloomy wood,
is the shifting of human shadows.
Further off, as a broad sword
shimmering under the rising moon,
a river extends along its undisturbed course
the rumours become more insistent.
And we distinguish 3 voices:

THE WARRIOR: No! No! No! I have never met a man such as this!

THE PRIEST: I must acknowledge, he has peculiarities.

THE MÆNAD PRIESTESS: He is more than peculiar!

THE PRIEST: That's the opinion among you Mænads?

THE WARRIOR: It is enough that he distracts people from fighting!

THE MÆNAD: Nae! He is strong. But so unreasonable ... There's that vagabond-child he returned with, from the bottom of the mountain ...

THE WARRIOR: The old madman's girl?

THE PRIEST: Well! Let's find her now.

THE MÆNAD: Why, he's took her as a wife!

THE PRIEST: How do you know ...

THE MÆNAD: I watch him, each night. Each night he passes by the river, always followed by her. He stops, he lies upon the banks, caressing, singing in a voice so powerful and so pure that any woman would yearn to be there—lying by him.

THE PRIEST: And how does she answer?

THE MÆNAD: She opens her eyes; she knows not what to say ... Another, more artful, would twig of how to make reply.

THE WARRIOR: You would like to be ...

THE MÆNAD: No. The air of magic is about him; he unnerves me.

THE PRIEST: He is no magician. The man is the King: the Oracle is veridical.

THE WARRIOR: I don't understand. Yet this much I see clearly: he does not make a good warrior: he will not make a good leader. When I threatened him, he fled; he fled to the deepest end of his lair. He's a caitiff! A coward despite his strength, his stature, his voice ...

THE PRIEST: Hush—we may be overheard—for as many ears as there be leaves lie around us; full, this wood, lain with rumours.

THE WARRIOR: Let them listen, let them murmur, be it so, that in telling, he might hear!

THE MÆNAD: May he not!

THE WARRIOR: Let him show himself; let him appear! I will say this to his singing face: you're not a true born leader! You'll never make a brave protector!

THE PRIEST: Listen, in the distance ... Hush, hush.

THE WARRIOR: Hush, hush! I'm always to shut up! Why

should I go quietly before him? Is he a man, is he a king, he, whose cares are only for the twitters of his throat?

THE MÆNAD: It's him! He's coming! The voice resonates like no other above the river.

THE WARRIOR: What can he be singing about now?

THE MÆNAD: Every night he commits a new hymn to the evening.

THE PRIEST:

Unbelieving

> How's it possible! He has compounded the strings of the lyre! He has strayed from the intervals; disfigured the venerable modes ... he invents his songs without the proper decorum.

THE WARRIOR: Wait, I mean to have my word with him too. Oh, let him finally show himself! Ah!

THE MÆNAD: He shines, effulgent even amid the light.

> *Further than the hostile forest,*
> *further than the rumours of men,*
> *further than the river bank*
> *walks* THE ORPHEAN KING
> *dressed in bedizened, dynastic robes.*
> *His LYRE he holds, raised before him,*

glimmering in the radiant light
of numerous strings, filled with sound,
shimmering in harmonial tone.

THE WARRIOR:
Advancing towards him

Hey you there! With the loud mouth!

From afar a murmur raises as of an unseen procession.
Under the wood, the RUMOURS grow.
We start to discern heads and shoulders
gesturing and grumbling.

RUMOURS: Hey there! You with the big mouth!

THE PRIEST: I knew it well, we were not alone.

THE WARRIOR: Ho ho! You, who pretends not to see ...

RUMOURS: Ho ... Ho ...

THE WARRIOR: Out of contempt, no doubt! You harbour contempt, huh?

RUMOURS: Look! Look! See for yourself!

THE PRIEST: Now it's all growling hostility ...

THE MÆNAD: Like wolves, from the shadows ...

THE WARRIOR: Hey? You who'd make out to be deaf?

RUMOURS: Open your ears! Open them well!

THE WARRIOR: Daren't you respond to insults?

THE MÆNAD: I have never seen him so proud and so noble.

THE WARRIOR: Hey, Lyre Man! Aren't you getting tired of holding it up so high?

RUMOURS: Lyre Man! Hoist it higher!

THE WARRIOR: Do you think you're a dove, to always go coo?

RUMOURS: Where are your loves, dove … your lovers?

THE WARRIOR: Hey you, swan who will not die, what have you done with your feathers?

RUMOURS: With your wings? With your neck?

THE PRIEST: This is their King—and they mock him! The King the Oracle pledged to be sacred.

THE MÆNAD: His breath would be enough to confound them—let them confront him: In the light, may they all reveal themselves.

THE WARRIOR: In the light?

Turning towards the crowd

Hey you there, Look!

And he rushes toward the KING,
followed by a charge of

PEOPLE, *exasperated*
at such a display of equitable serenity.
We suddenly see the WARRIOR
in full clarity, crushed by the fragments of song.
ORPHEUS,
patiently, indifferently, passes by.
The great voice did not so much as waver.
THE WARRIOR
stumbles in amazement,
stuttering toward the crowd:
He flees … he's … just a … caitiff …

RUMOURS: He flees … he's but … a … caitiff …

And still chattering, walking backward.
The curtain, falling, barely contains them.
The rumours diminish amid the running sound of
their feet.

(scene ii)

The curtain reopens.
We are on the bank of a river,
in the middle of the night, the moon is very high.
We see

ORPHEUS
lying on the bank.

EURYDICE:
Running up, frightened, before him

Where are you? Where are you? Do you not hear how they insult you, down there, braying at the bottom of the wood … (I've all their yelling ringing in my ears yet.) How've you not heard them?

You came by the same route that I have taken, past all the jeering …

Ah, but he's sleeping. Sleeping, in spite of them and me! Supine and tranquil, deeper, more gentle than he ever fell as he was held in my arms.

You leave me. You always leave me.
You are fleeing still. You are far, far away.

ORPHEUS: I hear you …

EURYDICE: Oh! the sleeper has spoken.

ORPHEUS: What is this astonishing voice? From where does she spring forth?

EURYDICE: I came this moment from the Palace, as you did.

ORPHEUS: Oh voice, so obscure ...

EURYDICE: No! it lies very close to you,

ORPHEUS: that I had found and lost ...

EURYDICE: She did not dare to ... She went mute ... Now, welcome me back, tell me that you'll keep me. Oh tell me, hold me, keep and console me!

ORPHEUS: Who is it asks to be consoled?

EURYDICE: Have those people, their insults, have they disturbed you? I hate them! That they dared to ... I hear them still ... Talk to me, so that I might forget.

ORPHEUS: She answers! She too hears. The dread silence will fall away.

EURYDICE: What is he dreaming? But his cares are not for me.

ORPHEUS: Are you there? Have you found me?

EURYDICE: Yes, yes, but now do not go again. Pray contemn me no more: I was a girl left so frantic then.

ORPHEUS: Listen to me.

EURYDICE
submits to all the desire and patience in his eyes.

ORPHEUS: Listen with me: Listen all the way to the depths to the world:

We hear a strange inhuman singing.

EURYDICE: What's there to listen for? I hear but the night. I hear only the water and the grass on the bank, the shuck of pebbles from the bottom of the river bed, the wind that falls, and the times that pass, the noises made by men who will. And then ... I can not hear more.

We hear again this strange inhuman singing.

ORPHEUS: It groans! It is afraid! It does not want to: The river comes rolling back on itself and stays there, suspended. Everything is collected and tense like in the theory of original chaos. And I! I am alone!

EURYDICE: He complains that it's he who's been abandoned!

ORPHEUS: O but I dance alone! But I fly alone! O that I must live all alone ... Why is this body still lain on the earth? No more am I in it. I swim among clouds of sound; I am ...

EURYDICE: He dreams more deeply yet. He surely is exhausted ... So pale ... He's barely breathing ... Now he breathes no more ... Orpheus!

> *The Name plunges the strange state and*
> *renders it as if a new corpus, in answer*
> ORPHEUS
> *doesn't shudder.*

EURYDICE: Oh fly; dance! Go where your spirit wills it!

> *Kneeling, plaintively beseeching*
> *by the chest of the sleeper ...*

I am here, faithful to your sleeping body, more pliant than any muliebral mortal has ever been ... Let some other jealous soul implore for caresses, the nubile consummation, I'm not here to ask for anything; I attend only, at the edge of your sleep. Yet never have you said to me what it is you love. Since the first, only did you sing:

"I love ... "

To what end?

Now he sleeps yet more soundly!
He's gone, he's lost to himself, far from this body that I hold under my fingers.

Go then! Go away!

No. Stay among the living.

Come back to me. I love you.

But I don't want you to dream anymore if I can not love your dream too! Ah!

She lies close by him binding the defenceless sleeper,
covering his face with her arms cradling and caressing him,
A shriek ... EURYDICE jumps back.

ORPHEUS
has opened his eyes.
All music stops.

LONG SILENCE
broken by the trembling voice of

EURYDICE: Forgive me ... I ...

ORPHEUS: I would this world be deaf and silent!

EURYDICE: This world ... But, where were you?

ORPHEUS: Who recalled me here? Who struck me?

EURYDICE: Oh no! Not me! She hurt me too ... this string broke and bit me so ... Though no one has touched her ... It snapped alone ... Though, so much the better; aye, then all the others!

That's the source from whence your scorn for me rises, her poisons surround you: it's her, your lyre!

I hate her: her power; how she possesses you, she has you, hexes you ... But I will deliver you. I will waken you always out of your terrors. So, that you may tell me of your love.

In a passionate gesture
ORPHEUS
takes up his LYRE
—reeling from EURYDICE:

You are beautiful and indomitable, Lyre, love enchanted! Guardian to the threshold of my sonorous palaces! Noble weft that weaves my sleep and protects my singing dreams. Lyre, it's to you that I play the games of love—

Your hips are polished and nacreous; the curve of your horn is arched like two dancing arms: Your voice is as numerous! Your sound so bold! When you shake, everything thrums and echoes. But, your nerves are live, now, here they break: the dead string drapes across my wrist and my fingers. What discord could have snapped it?

To be alone! Would you leave me so?
I'll take you away, delight with you, I'll have you, keep you, save you as myself!

He moves on downstream.

EURYDICE
bursts into tears.

The curtain falls brutally.
Eurydice's tears do not stop throughout the night.

(scene iii)

The curtain rises very slowly.
The night has
passed. A fresh mist from the river
gently drifts.
The moss and grass is frosted.
We are aware of the approaching dawn,
and the air trembles and laughs under
the breath of the new day.
Lying in the same place,
EURYDICE
moans to herself the same complaints,
but softer.

THE OLD MAN:

Appears.

He went further—further than usual during the night. It is here, however, that he comes back to sing. Oh, those snarling men prove themselves as less than animals—

Who could have thought to offend him more?

The old man nears

EURYDICE:
and she pleads with him

Father! Console me!

THE OLD MAN: Who is it asks to be consoled?

EURYDICE: Me, my father.

THE OLD MAN: What are you doing here? Why aren't you with him, you, only, he allows to attend.

EURYDICE: Woe, but he has fled me … left me, bereft me …

THE OLD MAN: He ran away from you!—What did you do to him, you nasty child? How have you upset … or disappointed him, perchance? Tell me: What have you said?

EURYDICE: I told him … that I love him …

THE OLD MAN: And?

EURYDICE: He fled me.

THE OLD MAN: You told him you loved him! Why issue words, so grossly misshapen, withered as they, by any hackneyed old woman?

EURYDICE: But I tried to please him—I strained to listen so hard to so much ... I forced my face and all of my thought ... All my being lay beneath his caresses ...

THE OLD MAN: Why appeal that he should treat you as his wife; he, who is other than any man; he, pendragon; more than any mere husband?

EURYDICE: O give me a man! A boar! A patronizing pig! Let him use me! That he should bind me! Smite me! That he might at least find to notice me!

THE OLD MAN: You do not know what you say.

EURYDICE: Ah, for you, you are satisfied with so little: Listening ... hiding in bushes ... Following his voice ... furtively ... stalking after him ...

THE OLD MAN: Daughter!

EURYDICE: And if, one day, he should show you his true contempt? If he were to mock you and push you away ... laughing with mirth ... singing as he went? How would you feel? What would you say then?

THE OLD MAN: My girl, settle down. Stifle up this spite. Save your love from reverting to the snide jeering of men ... What would I do?—I would lower my head beneath his disdain and I would follow his voice as it would abase me—and be present even to his silent contempt.

EURYDICE: You! You stay so lofty under defamity! Yet nobody has ever treated you like this—Nor have you so revered another entity—even the gods—as you do him.

THE OLD MAN: That's because He is nobody, nor even a god! One might approach him profanely and still his song would answer immediately. No, no, he's not some god descended—nor yet a god raised again. He's not as the men who have lived through the ages and equally is he confounded to live among us today. This is no anachronist; he is purely intemporal—atleast, if he is not of what is to come. The years that proceed for us cannot weigh on him.—That must comfort you, you my little wild one, daughter of the ravines, ever naked and naïve—He chose you, he followed you, he allows you sometimes, to his bed ...He fills you with an unexpected grace;—Better than in the old story you sung, of Semele-the-Blessed, who deigned to exult in the glory of the Great God Jove ...

EURYDICE: And who died ...

THE OLD MAN: Yes, yes, you remember.

EURYDICE: And ... if ... I ... am also to die?

THE OLD MAN: What are you thinking of?—You say so in a strange voice!

EURYDICE:

Tilting her head to the Old Man's knees

You console me. You can explain it to me. You draw up in me great resolve ... and fear also.

THE OLD MAN: Take heart, take heart. Do not be afraid. One does not just die of love, not among us simple folk. We can die no more of love than we can in sublime rapture. That may be beautiful, laudable ... Yes, that would truly be harmonious. Oh! But do not be afraid: No, we can not die like that these days.

The two remain, lost in thought, concealing a
prophetic dread.
Curtain.

III

The Portico and the Sea

In a
GREAT SILENCE

ACT III (only scene)

The curtain opens onto a whole room
of a Cyclopean Palace.

Harsh, falling straight from
a cruel yellow eye at noon,
the daylight flows
through a portico from which
one can see the whole of the sea as it lies silent, the

day rebounding from the solid surface of its liquid lead.
ORPHEUS
*leaning on the last column of the Portico, is not looking
toward the sea. He appears indifferent, uncertain …
However his vestments are made of great finery
as befits the King of a land whose wealth is drawn from
many mines.
Orphrey and gold damask his shoulder, his arms
and chest.
But his hair remains the same tone of pale bronze.
Slaloming, deftly
between the pillars of the entrance,
clinging to folds in the sheltering walls comes*

EURYDICE:
>   *Dressed as a sacrifice, or a wedding present.*

   I'm not scared; not anymore; not since my
   father has promised … Oh no, I'm not scared
   anymore—Not as all the Palace is—filled with a
   new angst!

He has stayed silent ever since the night that … And he is
silent still …

The fault is mine … It's me … Me alone has he chosen.
Should I keep on with following him further? Should I call
him again? I fear I have too often desecrated his name.
But might this be the decisive moment? Is this the instant
I need to act?—How to cross the great barrier of silence?

How to entreat; how to be received by him?

ORPHEUS:
> *In an almost human voice.*

Eurydice ... lost ...

EURYDICE:
> *Believing he has called, hurries to present herself.*

No! Is found ... all present ...

ORPHEUS:
> *Raises his eyes and regards her.*

EURYDICE:
> *stops, frozen under his hollow stare.*

... all ... present? But how can I approach you?
Each step is so thick through the silence ... The
heart weighs so heavy ... The knees buckle ... The
feet are rooted through the earth ... Oh! the
path to you is made languid and dolorous!

ORPHEUS: Why does *she* steal up to me?

EURYDICE: Accept me, you, having chosen me; you, who I
do follow ... who was waiting for me, by chance ... I heard
you call my name.

ORPHEUS: I called Eurydice, who is lost.

EURYDICE: I'm here. Observe me.

ORPHEUS: I called the mountain. I named the flowing river. I crossed the rumbling wood. I was looking for the unheard, the wild voice ... She did not hear my call.

Pause

Which no one could, over the noise of sighs and threats, of cries of death. She's done this! By what spell of feminine love?—Enough. I go quietly.

All around me is void. All within me, naught but stupor. That she be proud of her malicious, maidenly gall!

He turns away to look at the horizon, over the sea.

EURYDICE: May that he rather escape forever!

She is stunned and dazzled, she pleads comfort from all about her ... for relief from the harsh splinters of the sun ... into the shadows of the arches ...

But I was happy once, I was serene under the sun, out among the light ... I'd laugh to the new born day ... How this one burns without releasing my eyes, as so without rest, I cannot cry.

She dares to approach, by a wide, circuitous route, toward

ORPHEUS,

to regard, remotely, his expressions ... stumbling backward, as if walking in on a moment of horrific trauma:

Oh! you—but you are crying? So you can cry? You are a man ... Have you taken pity on me?

ORPHEUS: Be contented.

EURYDICE: You vitiate yourself for me?

ORPHEUS: So be contented!

EURYDICE:

Hesitant, hopeful, composes herself all of a sudden:

No! No! He is not the presaged prodigy

Hark!

This is not the revelation!

But observe me; recognise in me—I; Eurydice. Know that everything in her will awaken ... If you want it. Only ... Where is that Other? Is she abandoned as well? Is she also lost to you?—Master, degraded by my unworthy love, you—reduced to the file of common man—forgive me, forget me and take back up your lyre.

Restring your strength and joy—this companion incorruptible—without discord nor rancour. Go back to your den or higher—to the shelter, shelter in the skies.

ORPHEUS
little by little his face has changed, as increasingly he hears, seemingly not as one listening of the present but of the lyric flowing from the words to come.

EURYDICE: You're so far. You're so foreign ... yet you're neither a god come down nor the same resurrected?

Oh, if it is true that you make the mountain live to dance, if you finally deign to be our King, shake these vaults and pillars thus; that all the Palace be torn from the dolour that was brought about by your mournful silence—

Let all things resound! May the Palace obey! That it collapse and crush me if you can only regain your joy!

A ceasing. A temple of suspended exaltation ...
Then
ORPHEUS
reapprehending THE VOICE *from afar, as with a new hope:*

Who taught you? Who revealed that to you?
How do you know that I am not a god?

EURYDICE: My words do not estrange you? You hear me—so hear me: Vitiate yourself by me no more. Take back your power and your sceptre. Take up and bear your arms against me ... Use thunderbolts to lash me ... Cauterize and scathe me with light and with waves of pain. Lift up your Lyre ... Where is she?—Has she also gone clear?

ORPHEUS:
> *hesitant and almost panting:*

> There! ... that you are here ...

EURYDICE: Dare to understand the reason for the words that I say to you: I do not want you to turn away from her any longer ... I pledge to be her maid, I avow, I am ready. Let it burst out in a rain of gold or blood! I am her sacrifice. Master, take up your Lyre, back into your arms.

ORPHEUS:
> *Now suddenly unleashed.*

Why need I my Lyre ... with you here revealed?—You are Eurydice. You are the awaited harmony. Shall I dare, finally? Will I be able to realize everything?

> *Advancing on*

EURYDICE:
> *who instinctively starts to shiver.*
> *(aside)*

He can attain everything! As in the hymn that I sing, of Semele-the-Blessed ...

ORPHEUS: You are afraid suddenly: I saw you quiver.

EURYDICE: I'm not scared anymore, not since my father promised me ...

ORPHEUS: You first invoke my power then you tremble. You strengthen me only to buckle?

EURYDICE: No! No!

ORPHEUS: Are you afraid of some of the words? Or else the echo of those words?

EURYDICE: No.

ORPHEUS: You sang, "Let the Palace tremble and dance ..."

EURYDICE: Yes, let it fly if you have to ...

ORPHEUS: You sang that the earth may leap?

EURYDICE: Let it open! May she obey you!

ORPHEUS: Don't you fear that the air will quake, the air all in sound, the air full of flame; should it not burn you?

EURYDICE: Ah! that they burn me!

ORPHEUS: You are shaken with a hopeful anguish ... Hear how the fear has risen in your voice ... Tell me, what then are you afraid of?

EURYDICE: I'm afraid to disappoint you, O Master, or to be disappointed in myself. The moment I must live has come upon me, and I am afraid of that which will follow.

ORPHEUS: So be it! Listen! Oh Listen! Your desire is raising the song of the world: When I call, hear what rumbles. There!

EURYDICE: Something answers: a strange song, inhuman.

ORPHEUS: No ear has ever discerned it.

EURYDICE: Even though we'd fallen silent, even after the echo had ceased.

ORPHEUS: It's the Prodigy. The resonant breath of the abyss.

EURYDICE: The pillars and vaults shudder ... And they sound; they redound ... As by what magic, this?

ORPHEUS: By your voice finally unified to my voice.

EURYDICE: The earth responds! The land swells out and roars.

ORPHEUS: The Deaf rouses himself;—woken like a sleeper who has heard called out his name. He's rendered animate: he will sing from his million mouths.

EURYDICE: And I will hear it! Yet not enough to satiate my joy! Give—me more … I need everything. All, all to me. I want more. I want …

ORPHEUS: Let it so transpire.

EURYDICE: … to sing wholly under your voice … to sing under your voice like these stones! The ground is plangent, the air full of music—and I, alone in the world, would remain silent in this body that contains me!

Give me ashes or flames since everything is burning, is flaring!

Make me become a song that you love …

ORPHEUS:
                    steps back as if also afraid

EURYDICE: Be merciless: accomplish your work in me!

ORPHEUS: You want ... your flesh to resonate! You want ... to emancipate yourself of the body!

EURYDICE: Do not wait longer. There shall be no retreating now.

ORPHEUS: Eurydice!

EURYDICE: Already this is deeply sweet and beautiful.

ORPHEUS: Eurydice!

EURYDICE: You promised me an incredible marriage ...

ORPHEUS
responds, roars his first stentorian cry.

The amber light of the day is changed under its power to a vibrant luminosity that increases at each incantation which enters and dissolves all sight of the earth, the pillars, the arches and the sea.

EURYDICE: Ah! The Palace takes flight! The sea is boiling! What is this malleus glow?

ORPHEUS: Rejoice. The sun is afraid of us.

EURYDICE: I cursed it in my fantasy.

ORPHEUS: This is my singing dream.

EURYDICE: Without alarm! Without alarm!

ORPHEUS: Rejoice.

EURYDICE: Our voices answer each other.

ORPHEUS: The fell silence has been vanquished.

EURYDICE: Rejoice.

ORPHEUS: The world is sound!

EURYDICE: Orpheus!

ORPHEUS: The work is accomplished. The work is beautiful.

EURYDICE: The work is beautiful ... And I am faltering ... Orpheus ... under your voice. I'm only the echoes of your voice. I go. I am no longer ...

*She slumps and gently falls to lie in
ecstasy at the feet of ORPHEUS-REX
who, until the last, leads on with his inexorable hymn.
The two aligned, reign in this atmosphere
embraced with all music.
Everything is exalted in sonority.*

IV

The Temple Under the Earth and the Burial Chasm

*Aloud a desperate man cries
out—and the curtain opens.*

ACT IV (scene i)

*In stumbles the
OLD MAN
from stage left,
descending a paved ramp. By the light of
a tortuous day, we see it leads
into the vestibule of an underground Temple:*

My daughter is dead!

Then, from the depths of the hypogæum,
appear three SHADOWS holding torches
from which the flames splash against
the low, broad pillars that carry the interminable load
of the earth above.

My daughter is dead! What are you? Let me be—for dead, have I brought her, my only daughter, down here, where I sought to release her among the catacombs ... Who are you?

By the light of the torches, we recognize:
THE PRIEST, THE WARRIOR,
THE MÆNAD PRIESTESS

—Your daughter is dead? ...
—Dead, how do you mean she's dead? ...
—Dead, where is she? ...

THE OLD MAN: ... dead; died above, at the Master's feet, in the Palace of Sound. I found her there, outstretched, lain, as I said, at Master's feet; in rapture ... and I took her from there! I carried her away!

THE SHADOWS
surround the Old Man.

—Him?
—What was he doing?
—What did he say?

THE OLD MAN: He was singing, triumphant!

THE MÆNAD: He was singing, while your daughter lay dead!

THE PRIEST: Dead, what killed her?

THE WARRIOR: He has. He's killed your daughter.

THE MÆNAD: He could love her no longer.

THE PRIEST: She had to die for him.

THE MÆNAD: He found her unworthy of his wonder.

THE OLD MAN: Oh! Eurydice, my daughter!

THE WARRIOR: But tell us how she died.

THE OLD MAN: She died of an all-expanding love.

THE WARRIOR: Ho! The old fool!

THE PRIEST: One does not die of love, not among folk like us.

THE OLD MAN: I used to speak the same ...

THE PRIEST: She has died through malice.

THE WARRIOR: He's some formidable shaman.

THE PRIEST: It's sacrilege: he's not as mad as he pretends.

THE OLD MAN: Do not slander him. You haven't the dignity!

THE WARRIOR: And still you spring to his defence; oh good and faithful servant, even as he has killed your daughter. And while you are mourning, what is it that he is doing?

THE PRIEST: He has not grieved respectfully for this death.

THE MÆNAD: He neglects the funeral dirges for such a one as we love: Harken …

We hear a rustle of the LYRE.

THE OLD MAN: You! Oh! You will never truly hear.—He knows not of the death of my daughter. He yet is calling out for her! He wishes her, desires her. He is coming down to claim her, to take her back above ground, that she be with him …

THE MÆNAD: Here he comes! He's coming down! His voice will cause a shudder like naught beneath the earth before it!

THE OLD MAN: Praise be for *terra firma*!

THE PRIEST: But he would not dare descend further; down there …

*The priest makes a pious and fearful gesture
toward the extreme right: a bleak crevasse which
fumes forth curling vapours.*

THE WARRIOR: He needn't dare. I will force him in.

THE OLD MAN: Ho!

THE MÆNAD: This ... just could be ... the idoneous destiny that awaits him. As one forgets ... So he will forget ... And so be stripped of frenzy. He will become as the rest of men.

THE PRIEST: Let him go down, and may he never come out!

THE MÆNAD: Go now ... let me direct him. Let it fall to me.

THE PRIEST: Oh beware. It is fatal to all who approach. The crevasse is filled with mephitic vapour.

THE MÆNAD: Enough. Now snuff out your torches. He comes to me ... finally!

THE PRIEST: It is fair. He must atone for what he's done.

THE MÆNAD *slides into the mouth of
the crevasse. The torches are snubbed out. There
remains a horrible silence ...*

THE OLD MAN: What is this plot they've set for him now? What insult more hateful, abased and conniving?

Suddenly the great
VOICE OF ORPHEUS
roars into the underground temple.

THE OLD MAN:
throws himself before him to block his progress, beseeching:

O Master! Do not go down there! Cease your search! Run from them ...

ORPHEUS
appears.

THE OLD MAN: And run from me, even from me!

But we see and we hear
ORPHEUS
*passing through—crossing the
temple—plunging fast into the maw of the crevasse.
Suddenly the vapours boil and spit—
as if to reject the strange host that enters
and has yet disappeared inside.
Furious, the vapours continue to consume the scene,
forcing*
THE PRIEST, THE WARRIOR *and even* THE OLD MAN *to flee.
The effusion swells around everything,
engulfing the entire Hypogæum.*

(scene ii)

We find ourselves in an indescribable niche; this crevasse ...
this viscous cave, this pulp of a poisonous fruit ...
A manchineel ...
A few stray shimmers catch the crenulations and
fall around the rustlings of the LYRE,
—allowing for a little perception by which we see.

ORPHEUS:
frenzied, like a trapped animal

Further down! Deeper! Down to the impure belly of the earth ... I seek you in hysteria, O renegade!

Chasing and laughing! Groping my way! Searching folds of the strata that I had assumed were bare ...

Lower! Ha! And again further down, lower ... Men lose their souls amid such darkness!

I plunge onward yet! immerse myself in it! I'm sinking! Going down with delight!

The strumming of the LYRE
surrounds the words with violet sparks.

Are you there? Are you there?
Why would you disappear?

What has made you run away?

As answer, there rolls
through the mouth of the cave
the rebarbative echoes between THE OLD MAN *and*
THE OTHERS
—Dead ...
—Dead ...
—killed by him ...
— ... died by
—formidable ...
—Killed by
—malice!

ORPHEUS:

with anger

Dead ... Who said "dead"?

Bursting with a laugh of hatred:

These are those men ... up there! They squawk among
themselves ... Dead! They think that you're dead! But death
does not reach where we are.

A forceful thrum from the
LYRE leaves a gap between
rock and mire, sodden mounds, plunging
in to shadow from which comes back
an output of heavy vapours, soaking the ground

And from the depths of the cave, we see a
A FORM
unmoving, roughly veiled.

ORPHEUS: You are here: really! Amid this filth and all this silence ... Why? Why?

The light of the LYRE *penetrates the cave without illuminating it. And the sound and glow, extinguish under his redoubled anguish.*

You do not answer?

THE FORM: I am no longer the one you love.

ORPHEUS: Do not play with echoes.

THE FORM: I'm no longer the one you killed.

ORPHEUS: Do not make the echoes lie.

THE FORM: My voice is true.

ORPHEUS: Your voice is awry, suddenly ... What have you become? Eurydice!

THE FORM: I am not your Eurydice.

ORPHEUS: Such oration of ingratitude! That you would not be Eurydice! You believe in me no more ... Who might recognise you better than I? Answer!—You daren't? Your voice has defected, you are afraid of it yourself …

Yes. Best to stay silent … keep quiet … and then suddenly flee! Come back with me, to the Palace of Sound.

THE FORM: No! never again! Surrender all such hope! You are down here now as one who is dead. Ah! The sweet song of a mad bird! But he is choking … You are here below. You are a man. I am satisfied.

ORPHEUS: I am the Master. You will come!

THE FORM: You are now only master of the one hymn. A funereal dirge: as for the bride, so for the husband. I am contented.

ORPHEUS: You pronounce words without harmony … The sound of your mouth is barren … This is some vexatious mortal humour. These vapours, these plumes of stinking breath! This deaf, deathly crevasse … O! how can we fly, flee, be away from here?

THE FORM: None but I could reveal the egress. Nobody has come out from this place, not even a god. Yet I am ecstatic.

ORPHEUS: I gave you the fervour of my voice.

THE FORM: I've brought you to the Palace of my banns: Here lies the bed within the chambers. You crossed the threshold! The bride is revealed.

THE FORM *unveils herself.*

Orpheus! You must finally know and recognise me
—Look. It is I! The high Priestess of the Mænad! A
true virgin, like your Other, here, sacred before you!

ORPHEUS: Get away from me!

THE MÆNAD: I haven't touched you.

ORPHEUS: Eurydice, Eurydice, what have you become!

THE MÆNAD: Do not insult me.

ORPHEUS:

Hesitant.

What! You make florid suggestions ... like a harlot!
While your feet are bemired ever deeper in the
silage ... Your hands are defiled ... Haul yourself out
from this quagmire.

THE MÆNAD: This is my home! This is my eternal Palace. I
will have me that same fate as that Other did. Each night I
have envied her, there, at the river's edge.

It is also my desire ... Sing! You are ruthless to those who love
you—With all your power!

ORPHEUS: You crave ... (I do not understand you ...) I do not know what ... Wait ... It matters not! ... I must save you.

As a final recourse to an unwavering charm, He takes
up anew the LYRE and endeavours to make it ring.
The notes are stifled.

My LYRE is dimmed and choking ...

Even she is afraid to be here! Come! Follow, you, who I so followed ...

THE MÆNAD: I must obey.

ORPHEUS: I can not hear you any longer ... wretched, it is, to look on you. I see: you're engorged amidst the silt ... The tide of the mire rises higher round your legs ... The vault melts hot filth that rains across your breasts ... I ... can ... not ...

THE MÆNAD : Glory! You are here! You are mine! The lion will perish in my grasp;—so now, my captive, you must ravage me to death. You are my divine target! I would choose what god I love! He has come down to inhabit me, to render me to him.

ORPHEUS: What are you doing? You will drown us. I hear them laughing from up there. Their feet are stamping in excitement, they jeer above our heads! They are wild with the vapours, with the fire of our lament ... But no! They will not vanquish us: Remember, how we sang; how the Palace flew among the clouds ...

THE MÆNAD: You are in me. In my trap, my arms, my grasp. You are without strength and without voice …

ORPHEUS: I'm choking … I'm choking … This poison … This chaos … all in my chest … This fight is not mine.

THE MÆNAD: Glory! Within my Stygian Palace, to lie at the depths of my lair, come.

ORPHEUS: Help me!—No! Do not touch me so! This is no humane embrace about me.

THE MÆNAD: Enrapture! O what wonder! … Sinking in warm earth …

ORPHEUS: Who will save us! Oh, what use in asking?

THE MÆNAD: This is my bed of tenderness.

ORPHEUS: Do you think to evade the mud? Or …

THE MÆNAD: … the weight of the whole mountain …

ORPHEUS: … rather through shrieks of love, for the awful dance of bedrock and the vault …

THE MÆNAD: … is the fruit of my pleasure.

ORPHEUS: … be torn forthwith asunder! And we will sail amid the sky of my Eurydice.

THE MÆNAD: You have truly killed her. Yet she is not dead within you. Orpheus!

ORPHEUS: Do not commit my name in here.

THE MÆNAD:
>> *Calling out.*

>> Orpheus!

ORPHEUS: Cease!

THE MÆNAD: Yes. The silence. For both of us. There will be the same silence.

ORPHEUS: Come! Come!

THE MÆNAD:
>> *Through madness.*

>> I tell *you* to "Come"—I am the Queen of right here. I am high! I, Priestess, seize my God!

In a movement she embraces the upright figure of
ORPHEUS,
wildly, she grasps his hips.

ORPHEUS
tall and dignified, without flinching, raises his lyre above the tumult

and, taken with a loud laugh:

Ha! Ha! Ha! It's you who is doing this!
Ah! They were right up there; of your death,
for you are dead. You are not another Eurydice,
Death by love, dead up above.

... Yet I! Yet I! I raise my LYRE higher than all you can endeavour!

So! perish the woman!—LYRE, open me the fissure! The road to my salvation!

Loose me of this noxious snare!

With a shocking burst of power he tears the weft of the LYRE; the puncturing of the strings radiates the crevasse (which splits like a fruit), the Stygian thickness in the depths is traced in the flashes by which, in a single bound, escapes the vanishing
ORPHEUS
Everything collapses, crushing
THE MÆNAD
under an obscure chaos.

The Curtain closes over the darkness.

(INTERLUDE)

We follow through the ear the escaping trace of
ORPHEUS,
torn, desperate, parting;
dedicated and triumphal.
Thus, re-animating for mankind the possibility of
alighting from the underworld.
On seeing him reappear alive, there are
celebrations for this unexpected return of the King who
has vanquished Hades,
who has been resurrected from where no man has
come back human. Their chatter raises to shouts of
envy and amazement, melting and folding into the
path of the hero. They follow after him, the boisterous
tones persist above all else for a long time.
We join and we follow with the ear—we travel in
procession to the rebounding march
of ORPHEUS, *rewinding through the Drama*
as all the sound that was can be heard again:
Rolling back out of the Palace of Sound
still vibrating from the death of
EURYDICE,
Coming down to the banks of the
river, the rumours of the wood,
the trembling of his Lair ...

V

THE MOUNTAIN AMID
AN AOLEAN REVERBERANCE

And we go back with Him in calm serenity,
to the centre of the echoes at the first circulation
of the mountain—there, where scarcely an instant has
passed since
THE PRIEST *and* THE WARRIOR *elected their King,*
as accorded by the Oracle.

(EPILOGUE)

The curtain opens one last time.

Once more we see the pink conch shell of the mountain,
and,
nobly lain in the centre of the echoes

ORPHEUS
again alone.
His great voice and his LYRE's *numerous strings,*
restrung and tightened, are sounding at full soar ...
There swells a moment of radiance, a Hymn ...
But padding along at a hurpling gait
THE OLD ZITHER PLAYER;
He intimates that he wishes to speak ...

ORPHEUS: Do not disturb the echo of the Mountain.

THE OLD MAN: Forgive me ... You must listen to what I say:
You need flee again ... and further!

ORPHEUS: Do not interrupt the echo of the Mountain!

THE OLD MAN: It is not they who harried you before. Those men
have gone, they seek you no longer: they are far away from here,
involved in other schemes: I heard they kill each other over you.

ORPHEUS: Let them war.

THE OLD MAN: Or else they pretend you're an impostor. Or,
that you are indeed dead, but, as a god, resurrected.

ORPHEUS: Let them say it.

THE OLD MAN: They collect shreds of your tunic. They repeat
the words that you once sung. They mimic the pain of your
agony ... And they grieve.

ORPHEUS: Leave the men be!

THE OLD MAN: It's no longer men who threaten you! Hear what is coming now! Those who follow swiftly along the path of my own steps ...

ORPHEUS: No woman will ever join me again.

THE OLD MAN: No woman ... Yes, I know it, me, the Father ... Your marvellous strength: you are as terror redoubled to the ones who love you. You hold great power.—But all these ...

ORPHEUS:
Singing introspectively at half-tone, with a friendly demeanour:

Why have you never listened to me face to face?

Why did you not dare to whisper what you wished to tell me?

Take a breath, sing again, finally; sing according to your liking.

The intimation is so congenial and serene that
THE OLD MAN
forgetting his rush and his fears, sits, for once, having drawn near the Master.
Yes. I can now ... draw near you. Because something unites us and separates us.

At this moment, I can finally ask the questions of you:—Me. —Behold how you do not live like the men of today. Nor have you lived among those men who went before. You do not have the trappings of the venerated gods. You carry no age. You are nobody.

O but you! Then, who are you?

ORPHEUS: Orpheus.
The name echoes like light throughout the mountain.

THE OLD MAN: Oh! the Name thunders through the mountain! Worlds ... Open ... Too far! Too fast ...I'm too close to my time! Another will come, maybe ... Others will hear.

ORPHEUS: Confess me your second concern.

THE OLD MAN: Lo! Tell me without evasion—because I have a right to know—The one you ... who died below your songs by the force of the great love. The one that burned with ecstasy beneath your voice ... Out there, in the Palace of Sound ... Tell me, before her death under your song. Did she hear? She, who you have chosen, that you followed ... has she ...

ORPHEUS: I haven't followed anyone; I called ... I called ... Eurydice!
A sudden sough of

SMALL MYRIAD VOICES:
>*are everywhere, in the wind, by the tips of*
>*the branches, in the turning leaves,*
>*whirling, dangling drops*
>*suspended ... murmurate in Unison*

Eurydice ...

>*and the ravines, among the mountain,*
>*the attentive Sky enchanted with rushing softness*
>*on the Infinitude of*
>*this name ever multiplied.*

THE OLD MAN: Oh! Oh! I hear this: she lives: so she is immortal. Oh! Oh! It's more divine than to birthe a God!

THE SAME MYRIAD VOICES:
>*It's more ...*
>*divine ...*
>*than to birthe ...*
>*... a God!*

>*The engram, having penetrated the mountain, folds*
>*on itself, after relaying in*
>*circles towards* THE OLD MAN, *towards*
>ORPHEUS.

>*Both, in one common*
>*contemplation, extend to prolongate deeper into*
>*themselves the echo*

of this echo.
Respectful of each other,
Their songs lapse into silence and they exchange no
more.
But in the distance of space,
a hissing sound spears,
(THE OLD MAN stands)
So sour, so foreign, it seems astonishing;
the piercement of the formidable calm.
Another hiss ... and
suddenly, from everywhere,
We do not know how to discern where to listen ...
ORPHEUS
has not moved.

THE OLD MAN: Here they are! These are they! The Mænads in their fury, like rabid bitches ... They clamour for your death. To exact for that of their Priestess, crushed by your power; engulfed at the bottom of the crevasse ...

Do you remember?

ORPHEUS:
Remains impassive.
The whistles sharpen and reinforce themselves.

THE OLD MAN: Master! Master! Beware!

ORPHEUS: How can you find fear?

THE OLD MAN: It's for you. These harpies cannot be vanquished: they screech louder than anything: they whistle: they heckle ... They will tear your flesh away with their nails ... gnaw at you, scatter the pieces! Master, O Master, hear me one final time. Flee again! Evade them! You are not armed against this ...

ORPHEUS
Deigns finally to slowly rise. Swelling to the noble
posture where, first we found him singing,
He has his LYRE returned to his arms. His fingers set
And to the OLD MAN he smiles.

THE OLD MAN: Do you hold no disdain of death? So it is! You are the Master. But your voice! They are bound to reave that also ... Strangled it shall be ... Your voice will die along with the rest as all will fall to hollow silence ... Have mercy on those to come—your subjects. For the children of the sound world, Orpheus! Orpheus-Rex!

He bows, prostrate before
ORPHEUS
who slowly moves his LYRE
like a shield in front of his face ...
And the sounding mask,
gradually replaces his
human features.
In the paroxysm of the tempest, a huge wave
wild and white—of women,
innumerable, free and naked

adorned with the corpses of foxes:

THE MÆNADS IN FURY

leap, brandishing their sharpened reeds, cracking
their whips of vines and shaking their
sistras to this singular cry:
Tis him, this be the one-
—So see! He is the one-
—It's him, this be the one-
—'Tis he!'
and wildly assaulting ORPHEUS,
they overwhelm him, drag him, tear him apart,
deracinate him of his living voice.

THE OLD MAN

at first throws himself into the melee,
but is pushed away,
collapses, powerlessly
tries to crawl back.

THE MÆNADS *and their prey disappear.*
A black wave absorbs
all; and the scene is left clear.
We make out a

LAST SILENCE

then see close to THE OLD MAN *that*
THE LYRE, *whose*
shrieking, sparking song had
dominated the Tumult, is still lain where it fell,
neglected by the throng of assailants.

THE OLD MAN

raising his head, draws closer,
approaching, devout, reaches to grasp

it and take it from here.
In touching it
he fails, falls along side her, and so dies before his fate.
Alone, intact, deadly to all, beneficent, unreal,
harmonious,
THE LYRE
gradually ascends and hovers
beyond the abyss ... it
fulgurates in ascension; the song confirms itself,
and that's
THE FIRST VOICE
of ORPHEUS
—dominating through its epiphany over
the heavy earth, the woods and the rocks,
over love and play and cries; risen triumphally, it reigns
supreme.

END

∫

DRAWINGS AND
WOOD ENGRAVINGS BY G.D. DE MONFREID
1921

Synaesthetics and the Symbolist School[1]

As of long echoes, from afar, compound a
Unity, tenebrious and profound,
Vast as the night; and just as clear,
The perfumes, the colours, the sounds redounding
— Baudelaire, from *The Flowers of Evil.*

For a long time it remained respectable to advance, within the realm of science, a virtuous scepticism towards any possible correspondences between the interconnectivity of sensory perceptions. The indulgence stopped short only of a voluntary ignorance of the phenomenon altogether. A few were more rigorous. The doctrine of the Analogy of the Senses had its apostles, its martyrs, and quite recently its temple.

Vaguely occultist, exploited by the Adepts, it shared the discredit that is officially attached to all para-scientific notions. Nüsbaumer, at the beginning of the century, thus incurred academic wrath: his research in the field seemed unorthodox, and dangerous for its disclosure of certain facts—Benedikt, a professor and man of good counsel, imposed on him the silence of discretion.[2]

Trials continue, fumbling and hesitant. It seems that researchers are keen to apologise for their audacity. Thus, to avoid being suspected of credulity, they pose their efforts ironically. And the defiant prefixes with which they dress their suspicious definitions are curious to note: '*Pseudo*-chromaesthesia,' says Chabalier. '*Pseudo* photaesthesia,' says Suarez de Mendoza ... '*False* sensorialisms' ... '*Illusions*.' One doesn't want to be compromised.

In reality, appearances permitted for doubt and excused ambiguity.

The best-intentioned observers encountered a manifest incoherence, a disappointing failure in finding any general conclusion from their studies. Despite all their good will, it is difficult to hand over the keys to the City of Impersonal and Objective Science for such a phenomenon whose *subjectivity* itself is its rule, and for which the only possible criterion is an affirmation that the experimental proof required has yet to be found.

Currently, however, with the *aggregate* of examples painstakingly piling up, the evidence for the existence of synaesthesia is no longer doubtful. A civil partnership has been formally recognised. Among the scientists, these bastard-outcasts have found a legitimacy; they have been acknowledged.

§

A history.—Down through the ages, long before arriving here, synaesthesia has gently wandered through the mind's imaginings.

From the Vedic period, Hindu poets used, as their basis, three modes of Poetic Expression. Of these modes, the most elaborate is designated precisely by the word 'DVANI' (sound, repercussion). Fifty centuries before our Symbolists, sensory correlations had found their literary application.[3] The entire and mysterious word of the Hebrews was 'יהוה,' IEVE,[4] and this single word contained all Science. Then, initiates attributed to each of its letters a specific colour. These coloured phonetics weren't waiting around for the famous *Sonnet des Voyelles* to illuminate the Kabbalah.[5]

From there, without stopping for Classical civilization, whereby the Muse of Reason would tolerate few such subtleties; continuing until the late seventeenth century when there was a conscientious rejection of antiquity so that we might find, in the eighteenth, the tentative application of the phenomenon that had remained, until then, pure speculation. It is no longer a Mystic but a Jesuit who explores the subject. Father Castel imagined his 'ocular harpsichord' (1759). The theories of the good Father are incoherent and his comparisons puerile: *Blue* is the tonic 1st, in the 'Scale of Colours,' because *black + white* equal *grey-blue* (?). The *Red* is the dominant 5th: no explanation this time. In practice, it is a complicated instrument: five hundred lamps, sixty coloured glasses ... alas the great Cavaillé-Coll had no need to reform the manner in which he built his organs; the result was deplorable. But the sweet inventor had faith: 'Who knows,' he asks, with an emphatic gesture, 'if the ocular harpsichord will not be placed by posterity amid the ranks of the new arts that have contributed to the Glory of the Century in which we live?' The idea was full of philanthropy: Father Castel dreamed of a music 'for the usage of the deaf.'[6]

In the absence of intellectuals, the artists persevere. Goethe (*Theory of Sounds and Colours*)[7] does not remain indifferent, Gautier (articles in *La Presse*) finds there to be correlations within the transient raptures of hashish, and notes the artistic value. The virtuosos and musical technicians make gains therein—(Joachim Raff, Louis Ehbert). Auditory-colouration travels to London for its scientific baptism (*London Medical Record*, December 1882) and seems to have returned as definitively orthodox. Its heroic days were over. Suarez de Mendoza devotes a conscientious monograph to it. Millet, a naval doctor, introduces the precision of statistics. Theses multiply. An excellent work by Destouches highlights its possible adaptations to the practices of art.

We refer you, for all details, to the cited works. We will attempt to simply outline what logically acceptable deductions make synaesthesia a powerful—yet intimate—means of art—a prodigious tool—though strictly for personal use—the effective and benign stimulus which the poet's mind has ever summoned to express the New, to catalyse creativity; a tool utilised, in a word, like figurative forceps, a midwife for the sometimes painful birthing of new Beings into the world of the Ideas and Sensations.

§

Examples and Theories.—Two by two, they go, randomly juxtaposed with what different information our sensory perceptions provide. We must therefore consider both our surroundings and ourselves. Let's go through the peculiar conditions.

The results will be, at first glance, for the uninitiated, unexpected and improbable if not inconceivable and grotesque. Every malady that can create a mental delusion through teratological conceptions has accumulated herein. Hence the defiant attitude common to the first explorers of these cerebral regions toward the oppressive atmosphere of disorder.

That Rimbaud says an 'A' is black; that Meyerbeer considers as 'purple' certain strains in the music of Weber; this is still, to simple souls, tolerable. We already leave so much to artistic licence! ... But here is where the paradox begins: 'Pluck a guitar, and immediately we see a coloured image that surrounds the vibrating string,' says an Auditory-colourist.[8]—'Sunday appears to me *pale grey*,' said Diamondi, the prodigal mathematician; 'Monday, light brown ...' and the polychrome extended all week. For others it invades the calendar.

Then the taste sensations get involved. The olfactory stimuli rise to the top: 'Kirsch rings, furious as a trumpet; gin and whiskey take to the palate with strident bursts from the pistons of trombones; brandy fumes with the deafening din of tubas.'[9] Finally, a last consideration; materializations acquire defined shapes: a particularly talented subject saw 'couch-shaped prayers'[10] and the adverb 'where' covering the outline of a map of France. Geometry and abstraction exist there as themselves: and, to *such* a spirit, *specific* sensations coalesce into the appearance of a system, a diagram which always constructs itself in the same peculiar way.

So everything is possible, in the world of synaesthesia: even the most unforeseen sensory puns, and the most monstrous connections. But here, from the chaos, we can identify some generalised notions. In our examples we will confine ourselves to Auditory-colouration, which is the most extensive, and the most frequent of synaesthesia.

We'll use the term 'Primary' for the point-of-departure sensation, objectively *perceived*; and 'Secondary' for its concomitant, its Echo; the sensation thus *induced*.

The psychological mechanism of association seems to us, as it did to Destouches, to fall into the two following categories:

Category A. The Secondary sensation is *objectified*, that is, 'it possesses all the characteristics of intensity and externality apparent in a true perception. It is projected and localised externally, like a hallucination, and mixes with the sensations that are really experienced to the point of not being perceptibly separate.'[11]

In systemising, we would say that the letter U, for example, definitively *appears* green; that the key of C major is *seen* white.

Category B. But the Echo sensation can be simply a thought, existing only in the state of Ideation, and its relationship to the Primary is that of analogy, rather than an actual evocation. Following this example, we could say this time that the letter U makes one *think of* green; that the tone of C major carries an *apparent* pallor.

Between these two extremes, any degree of intensity is possible 'from the vivid apparition whose energy rivals almost that of external perception, to the vague and elusive glow hardly deserving to be called an image, confined purely within idea.'[12]

So far, nothing that is analytically verifiable by observation. But here is where the hypothesis begins. Two theories, one psychic, the other physiological, dispute the authority of the phenomenon:

'Mere *association of ideas*,' suggest some.

'The *entanglement* of nodes, of nerves or at least an intra-nodal overflow,' answer others.

Also, the two explanations could simply overlap and need not be mutually exclusive. Readily we would insist however, on the key tenet that was neglected by the English associationist school—that of *affected repercussions*. Two ideas, even if fundamentally dissimilar, such as a visual image and an auditory perception, are equivalent, because both produce in us the same *subjective reaction*; because they have, we would say, the same *emotional tone*.

§

Artistic value of synaesthesia.—While science began gropingly to risk the study of these subtle correspondences, a whole school felt its fecundity, making good use of it within their aesthetic and material processes. The Naturalists proclaimed their rights as observers, Symbolists affirmed with equal energy the artistic value—the expressive force of sensory correlations. The famous sonnet of Rimbaud, *Sonnet des Voyelles*, was a little manifesto for the new belief:

A black, e white, i red, u green, o blue, vowels.
I will tell some day of your latent births ...

And René Ghil, with imprudent zeal, became its outspoken apologist, extolling a liturgy for the artform, as its Neo-testament.

Here, once again, irony got mixed in with it.

The sonnet of Rimbaud, who was himself, for that matter, a paradoxical man,[13] is really apocryphal, both in intent and meaning; such is according to the author's own admission: 'To me,' he begins in his *A Season in Hell* – 'to me, the story is one of my *follies* ... I invented the colour of the vowels ... I regulated the forms and movement of each consonant, and set them to instinctive rhythms, I flattered myself, that I'd invented a poetic language, accessible, someday or other, to all the senses ... I wrote the silences, the nights, I jotted the inexpressible, I captured Vertigo ...'

'The text is clear,' says Kahn. 'The sonnet of the vowels contains less of an aesthetic than it does a dare, a prank to amaze the bourgeois. Rimbaud went through a phase in which, affected by poetic novelties, he sought a register for the phenomena of Auditory-colouration that he'd gathered from some rudimentary science of sonorities.— He was living near Charles Cros, at that time fixated with his experiments in colour photography and who directed Rimbaud toward research of this nature ... Yet there remain, tentatively, some beautiful analogies noted within the verses of his sonnet.'[14]

But before all that and above any other poetic attempt, one profound artist has, as Precursor, used the new technique astonishingly. And far beyond the pleasant sonnet of Rimbaud, the *Correspondances* of Baudelaire remains the primordial initiator of similar attempts:

CORRESPONDENCES

Nature's a temple of living pillars,
That sometimes let out a pledge confused;
Man passes on through forests of symbols,
Observed, as beneath the regard of familiars.

As of long echoes from afar, compound a
Unity, tenebrious and profound,
Vast as the night; and just as clear,
The perfumes, the colours, the sounds redounding.

It's fresh, the scent, like an infant's flesh,
Sweet as an oboe, green as a meadow,
—Then others, corrupted, rich and triumphant,
Carry expansions of infinite things—
Like amber and musk, resin and incense,
Which sing transportings of the spirit and senses...
(*The Flowers of Evil*)

This is really the initial impulse that has since haunted its disciples. Such associations, moreover, would clearly fall in harmony with Symbolist tendencies, and resounded in minds drawn to the subtleties of using this analogous method in a shared sense of a potent and serene beauty. Indeed, we find ourselves aware that associated sensations emerge other than as glib juxtaposition; the echo-sensation is not only evoked by the Primary, but is, at the same time, fertilized ... It gives birth to a youthful emotion, vibrating with freshness and unexpected renewal.

But exaggerations were not long coming. By complicating them, they wished to send up, for public spectacle, the processes which hitherto had remained personal. The Theatre of Art[15] chose, as a theme for such an attempt, Salomon's *Song of Songs*. To 'synthesize the mood of the dream,' the auditory sense, sight and smell were all engaged.—The agenda was: 'First positions—orchestration of the I sound, luminescence of the O, orchestration of the music in D; colour: In light orange; perfume: In pale violet.' The olfactory part of this orchestration was practically entrusted to vaporisers placed in the wind instruments.

The result was a disappointment. Sarcey, disturbed, was heard uttering loud moans.

Another collective attempt: 'We already have the arts of colour (painting and its derivatives)' says Mr L. Favre,[16] 'and the arts of movement (poetry, dance, music of sounds), can we not, by borrowing what can be taken from the arts of colour and movement, produce an art that combines the aesthetic effects resulting from these various sources?'

Alas, no. At least, not at the present stage of our sensory evolution. All correlation is purely subjective and exclusively personal. And the only general fact is the impossibility even of their generalisation. Some see *yellow* as the timbre[17] of a horn, that of the flute *blue*, *green* for the oboe (Lavignac, *Music and Musicians*). For me, the horn is clearly *purple*, the flute *opalescent* and, during the orchestrations of Gevaert, the oboe appears as a red line. There is similar variance in relation to the colours of the vowels. Millet, in a clever move, endeavoured to reduce these fleeting whimsies to statistics and to detect amidst the disorder consensus through majorities. The polling obtained for different vowels remain doubtful; A is *black*; unless it's *white*, *red*, or *green* ... That's all we can say.

Disagreement is thus the rule: The Nüsbaumer brothers, both convinced Auditory-colourists, did not get along on this subject. 'The red, which, for one, harmonized perfectly with the A, gave the other the impression of a 'counter-sense,' of a 'false note'.'[18] Thereupon begun their disputes. One discerns the general war that would spring up between all people over such discordances ... It is perhaps in anticipation of such a possible fray that the wise Benedikt, previously quoted, advised against the very study of such phenomena.

Much better. It is no longer from one individual to another that disharmony is sometimes asserted, but in the divisible intimacy of the very same participant. The imprecision of the phenomenon is therefore often as flagrant as its subjectivity: ask an Auditory-colourist about a watercolour—witness their colour-phantasms. Then, putting the watercolour aside, ask the subject to pick out the same colours from any chromatic chart, that of Lacouture, for example, which contains 600 typical hues. Result: Designations are only consistent as broad swathes of colour, not in subtle tones. 'We notice the same disparity between two coloured alphabet paintings made by the same person a year apart.'[19]

Some even admit to the fleeting sense of these impressions. 'I cannot indicate with any degree of nuance, the colour that corresponds to such a sound; the A pronounced with a sour accent in Montmartre or Montagne, does not have the same colour as the one in pâtre ...' writes Mr Binet, another Auditory-colourist.

Sensory synaesthesia cannot be of any public use. *Subjectivity*, the essence of these phenomena, restricts the use of the *subject* itself; rigorously, without possible escape from its personality. It cannot yet be a means of collective art, no matter how refined the supposed chosen circle who are to receive communion therein, and no matter what specific training that this elite has undergone. The music of Colours, Fragrances, and Flavours can only exist as egoism or musical research. 'Popular Concerts' would migrate thus only under martial law.

Nevertheless, a profound artist will know how to utilise these states to illuminate their work. Against the sensations brutally defined, they prefer delicate suggestion, rocking the personal dream of each listener.

They have reduced the relationships to two sensations, held within the Book, rather than hoisted up on stage; they do not distribute programmes. These are, naturally, the ear and the eye, as the most educated of our sensory devices and the first to be put into service. And here are the results.

Some examples, to start with. The title, structure and symbol of the work must reveal or evoke its secret essence. Now, Stuart Merrill writing his *Gammes*, Jean Moréas his *Cantilènes*, Adolphe Retté making *Bells Ring in the Night*,[20] and across the entire oeuvre of our sweet Verlaine, finer than any music sung or from the strains of *Song without Words*.

This surge of rhythms and timbres is characteristic. The century of the Sun King had seen an out-pouring of architects in various arts, Boileau as Le Nôtre[21] ... and the gardens of Versailles share a definite aspect with the *Art of Poesy*:

... correct, ridiculous and charming (Verlaine).

Painters became Romantics; from their truculence we have Delacroix. But music, having taken off as a profound and poignant expression of all humanity, subjugated symbolism:

Music before anything else,

—sings Verlaine. Later, he cries wildly:

O Music, again and always...

And the cry was heard. Drawing from the polychromatic legacy of the Romantics, today's poets have mixed polyphony with their own flexible rhythms. ' ... That's enough!' says Saint-Pol-Roux, though himself a grand master of such artifice—'Just open a book and they will squirt you in the face with words, elicit a display of stinging insects, still alive enough to emancipate themselves from their pins; and in various colours, such as of a feather, dipped hither and thither in the rainbow; these marks should be left to amaze me in the salons of painters rather than here, in my chair, within the pages of our best writers! And perfumes! And flavours! Scrawling a deviant orchestration. A prestigious delirium! Ah! It is no more the form in itself, but its essence, its wash, its model, its echo, its odour, its shadow, at least, the phantom of such a form!'[22] And further on: 'In writing, through an abundance, I proceed symphonically, perching the words on staves for instruments: Here are the strings and the woodwinds, here the brass and the drums.'

But each composer has his favourite timbres: Massenet chooses the warm tones of the cello and Reyer the flushed accents of the horn. In Saint-Pol-Roux, his atavistic visions remain magnificently bright and brutal,[23] as he, 'despite the melancholy of exile, persists in rendering the sun.' Brass dominates; his oeuvre is entirely a Fanfare of Colours. The great dawn is already, for him, advancing, personified by angels 'emptying their cheeks of snow into *trumpets* of the sun'[24] and the black night has

> ... the moon, caught suddenly
> In an opaque cloud the colour of sin
> A lofty pavilion for his luciferous horn ...

But two years of Breton horizons nuanced the semi-tones of his primitive orchestration, and enriched his composition with softer timbres: 'The Image of a penny, the Colour of smallpipes, a village, a rustic village where the bells seem to swing from the neck of a huge stone goat ...'[25]

And there's a horn encore that sounds like Stuart Merrill's *Gammes*:

Let aspiration hatch;
Clamour at the heart of a red clarion,
In a Blue apotheosis:
Glory be to all sweet and fervent lovers!

... And brass, finally, that evokes the following stanzas—metallic—of our friend Pierre Richard: The epigraph, to begin,

Tuba mirum spargens sonum[26]

preceding a description of the burning West, which is already a synaesthesia. The first quatrain specifies the correlation:

The brass of evening rang long calls
And the metal on fire dripped in the sky
Covering the clangour; the ephemeral songs
Of Dream...

Then the image is transformed and becomes Apocalyptic:

So sounds the *buccin* of the unwavering Archangel
To evacuate the dead before their coming hour of Judgment,
Load anguish to their heart, so awoken, without mercy
The sinister fanfare's strain into the coruscating evening ...

But everything blurs and drifts off in a twilit murmur:

Then all notes deviate – darkly, as well as bright,
Its vibrancy the paler where less bitter is the night,
An oblivion of sleep in the Lands of Illusory,
We drift in repose of a wish, for all eternity.

This same moment of the declining lambent, another of our friends—André Demelle—saw with less clamour: less of copper—a new amalgam of bronze:

... The sea – this molten green of Venetian shade,
As the setting sun, darkens down—becomes
An infinite bell of bronze – with thunder's thrum.
(*Glaucous Symphony*)

The auditory sensations are not only evocative of coloured visions, but also of Forms, Figures and Geometric Schemes, from which colour should be totally absent.[27] Such Photisms[28] are now perfectly demonstrated, and to their study we would like to introduce the somewhat nebulous notion of the 'shape' of sound:[29] Bleuhler and Lehman recognised that high pitches often evoked in their subjects a series of acute angles. The bass sounds, more blunt, dull, became arcs and geometric curves. All this might seem material only for engineers, not for poets, elements of serious architecture and not literature.

Yet here is what the subtle craftsman and goldsmith J.-K. Huysmans draws:

A song both slow and desolate rose, O the 'De Profundis'.
Sheaves of vocals spun under the vaults, fused with the

almost green notes of harmonicas, left the sharpened timbres of crystals broken.

Held on an endless drone of the organ, supported by so hollow a bass that it seemed as if it had lowered through itself, gone underground, to burst forth again in chanting verse.

And after a pause, the organ, assisted by two contrabass, roared, carrying on a torrent, all voices, the baritones, tenors, and bass, no longer servile now, but as youths who unsheathe sharp blades, go sounding, untrammelled, giving force in full cry, and the elan of the petite soprani pierced them everywise, crossed them, like a crystal arrow, in a single arc ... Suddenly, at the end of the psalm; the voice of innocence, torn apart. A vicious shriek of silk, in a *sharpened* sob, trembling over the word *'eis'* which remained suspended amid the void ...

These clear and sharp voices, in the darkness of the song, set whiteness abroad throughout the dawn ... [30]

And he continues, magnifying the plainchant whose melodic harmony, through medieval architecture, is so rigorous, and which, for him, sometimes 'bows like sullen Roman arches,' sometimes 'arises tenebrous and thoughtful, as does a *plain parabola* ...' the *'De Profundis'* for example; 'curved like those grand vaults that form the smoky frame of an arcade; it is slow and nocturnal like they are; it only stretches out in the darkness; would only move in the sombre obscurity of a crypt.

And still there are the oppressive forms of lower arches evoked by the '*Dies Iræ*', the medieval hymn of despair, turning 'dolorous alluvions in time.'

A basso profundo, *vaulted* as it bowled from the caverns of the Church, underlined the horror of the prophecies; compounding the stupor with menace.

From the dryness of lines and curves, from the diagrams and abstractions of space, here comes a procession of new images, an ordered, coherent series of *literary figures* that do not have, as sole *raison d'être*, their beauty and novelty, but respond to the real modes of associated thinkers.

Let's now reverse the terms. From Auditory-colouration, let's move on to the evocation, through colour, of a phonic sensation. The phenomenon is rarer, and rarer also is its artistic use. Léo Delibes used it finely in the orchestration of *Lakmé*, where the two flutes, in unison, emphasise, in the arpeggio by a diminished seventh chord, the evocation of the sharp gleam of a dagger.[31] In the same vein, any imitative rhythm: the *Ride of the Valkyries*, *Siegfried's Forge*, the persistent descent of the basses in the *Twilight of the Gods*, the long 'glissando' of the harp accompaniment in *Parsifal*, the whistling trajectory of the spear thrown by Klingsor.[32]

And we would say, yet more synthetically still, that the leit-motif itself, the powerful means of musical expression already considered by Gluck, then summoned by Wagner to express the inexpressible, can ultimately be defined: a synaesthesia where one of the sensory terms would be replaced by an abstract term, a character, a fact, a principle

... playing the role, for the author, of the Primary sensation. As for the Secondary, it is none other than the musical outline itself which embodies this character, this principle, this fact. The leit-motif is a 'Personification.'

But the two terms can remain exclusively literary ' ... Have I not found myself,' said Saint-Pol-Roux, subtly, 'coming to offer an arm to a verse of Henri de Régnier, to court a sentence of Griffin, to praise the prose of Mallarmé, to kiss a maxim of Mæterlinck, to pick out a song from Kahn, to quaff a sonnet of Verlaine, to sand a litany of Remy de Gourmont, to eat a sketch by Huysmans?'[33]

The sense of smell, for some so evocative of memories, is, in the human species, still too obtuse and insufficiently refined to be truly objective in precise terms.[34] Somewhat vaguely, Guy de Maupassant writes: 'I did not really know if I was breathing music, *hearing perfume*, or sleeping in the stars.' Hoffmann further specified: 'The perfume of the dark red carnation acts upon me with extraordinary and magical power. I fall involuntarily into a swoon, and therein I hear, as at a great distance, the sound of a horn spill and weaken, little by little.' But the 'Olfactory-Sound' still awaits its virtuoso. 'Aural-Gustation', however, had its technician and performer in the fictional Jean Des Esseintes.[35] What musical instrument manufacturer will be responsible for producing the subtle 'organ for the mouth' that Huysmans composed at the time of his 'Treatise on Harmony or Counterpoint,' where the Bénédictine liqueur is, so to speak, the minor tone in the key of alcoholic major, when the score designates a quaver of a green Chartreuse? And what travel guide, in a special edition for 'Ocular-Gastronomers,' will note the esculent impressions of our great networks, with the same spirit Saint-Pol-Roux did for the Paris-Marseille express ... completing the pantagruélesque dinner of the 'Glutton-Eye' with 'cup of coffee tunnels'—that follow the 'bright cognac of the reappearing sun?'[36]

Less likely to find literary use are the lower manifestations of our sensorium—tact, electro-aesthesia, muscular memory—whose receptive organs—peripheral neurons— are still so barely specialised. Note, however, the 'symphony of small soft sensations' that the acute intoxication of opium can invoke across the entire surface of the skin. But the colour sensibility that Dr Le Dantec has championed scientifically[37] has never been, we believe, attempted as it might apply to art.

So far we have assumed that the second term of our correspondences is necessarily an image. But this term can be abstracted, leaving the domain of the senses, and, by a sort of intimate levitation, become a feeling. As to which science, subtle and exacting, lies behind these Analogies of this further level, it is that of *Semiotics*. The symbol is the substitution, at the Primary term, of the element evoked by that term. The leit-motif is an example of such a specialised symbol.

The term Primary can be well understood. It is the current and concise form, obscured though it sometimes is, by way of subjectivity. But often two elements are expressed: Thus, throughout the *Orisons of Evil*—a sort of delicious and perverse *Way of the Cross*, from which each station proceeds out of a Jewel—the stanzas unfold and are closed off with subtle allegories of feeling. The lapid images—themselves derived from carnal visions—engender to themselves a mystical symbol, scrupulously appropriate to their legend, their reflection, their 'crystalline personality.'

> May your hands be blessed, for they are impure!
> They hold a secret sin at every knuckle;
> Lily is the dread evoked by the Nails, white beneath the lamp
> Of spirits stolen out of the shadows, white beneath the lamp
> And the captive opal that is dying on your finger-
> It is the last sigh of Christ, racked to the cross.

So Opal—sad, despondent Opal, evoking only agony ... For a Sapphire, this is

> ... painful; O sapphire of fearful bitterness,
> This is the last glance for Christ, racked to the cross.

And Jacinth, still more tender yet

> ... with a sad eye lain across the king,
> It is the last love of Christ, racked to the cross.

Then Topaz, shivering,

> This is the last desire of Christ, racked to the cross.

> ... And this cruel ruby, all ruddy and cold,
> This is the last wound of Christ, racked to the cross.

Finally, Amethyst, benumbed amid bereavement:

This is the last thrill of Christ, racked to the cross.

Then, the symbolic procession, having been liturgically unfolded through the triple correspondence of carnal visions—precious stones, the final agonies of Christ, and then, as trinity, it reaches the World of Ideas:

> May your soul be blessed, for it is corrupt!
> Proud emerald fallen to the paving of the street,
> Its pride mingling with the scent of mud,
> As I'll be crushed in to that glorious dirt
> On the paving of the street, for such is the way of the rood;
> The last thought of Christ, racked to the cross.[38]

All these examples necessarily imply two terms: the poet, the creator of the association, and his reader, for which the latter can infer, or not, its repercussion. It is still too externalizing for such idiosyncratic states of mind. Here then, are some rigorous cases where their use remains scrupulously subjective.

Secondary apparitions can, above all, be modes of control, directing one sense through another: A baritone who was an Auditory-colourist had, according to Mr Grüber, the recourse to chromatic visions that allowed him to distinguish between the finest nuances of his voice.[39] Thus, they can have mnemonic uses: such a musician, by colouring the notes, can supplement, through visual memory, for an insufficiency in his technical memory.

But above all, it is permissible, in these Analogies, to see fertile and powerful means of *cerebral excitation*. Each artist has their favourite vice, which they take, at times of mental collapse, on the sluggish march through ideas and which arouses, in moments of intellectual darkness, an inspiring flame: Nicotine, alcohol, the excitation of bright, strobing light, caffeine, opium and hashish all have their curious adherents who implore of them through systemic use to bring about a cognitive leap.

Of the same rank as these mental poisons, but incomparable due to their harmlessness, are placed the aesthetic synaesthesias—genuine *Alkaloids* in the chemistry of ideas, essential oils, effectual, toning, both spiced and dynamic nourishment.

Previously, in the early years of the century, Salomon Landolt, magistrate, painter and musician, admitted that, because of his relationship to chromatic scales, he 'was disposed to pleasant provisions of colour which greatly facilitated him.'[40] Fournoy knows of a painter endowed with Auditory-colouration who, when vision deserts him, takes up his violin 'and finds in the sounds of this instrument the hues and nuances that his picture demands.'

In the aforementioned pages of *En Route*, geometric visions served J.-K. Huysmans as a *framework* for drawing an architectural plan of a coherent edifice. The colouration of musical tones may be of similar use in composition. The auteurs who benefit from it have doubled their sources of inspiration. Thus, once the harmonic idea has been born, it is, it seems to us, a valuable support on which to erect the tension, the coherence and the meaning required for modern works of art.[41]

∫

Synaesthesia is not a symptom of degeneration but progress. The synaesthetic processes are thus being posed as initiators to an entire school—Symbolism; and of an entire movement—Wagnerism, or 'Expressive' music generally. Thus, Mr Max Nordau has been incited to extend his indictment, his accusations against the state of modern art. For him, this was the crown jewel; because to make the morbidity felt, to convince them of their defects, to summarily catalogue them to the general directory of Degeneration, was to, in a single stroke, consign every participant off to the hospital, if not the asylum.

He did not miss his mark. His 'atavistic' theory of Auditory-colouration is among the least flattering. Having repealed and dismissed Rimbaud's whimsical sonnet, he severely critiques the anachronistic zeal of René Ghil and Francis Poictevin, before making a leap back to the states of prehistoric souls, back to an antediluvian state of mind, and casting a glance over the psychology of molluscs:— The clam, for example, has, as its only sensory apparatus, a siphon, but a siphon remarkably endowed, 'sensitive to all external impressions, light, noise, contact, scent.'[42] The animal in question 'thus sees, hears, tastes, and smells with this single part of the body; his siphon thus serving as, at the same time, an eye, ear, nose and finger.'[43] This, for Nordau, was the first stage of the human sensorium. In the course of evolution, each perception has, from this magma, differentiated, so as now to constitute each of our sensory organs. Yet, says Nordau a little harshly, the Symbolists 'claim to perceive mysterious relationships between colour and sensations from their other senses, the difference being that they hear the colours, whereas he (Baudelaire) felt them, or, if we like it better, that they have an eye in their ear [!] whereas he saw with his nose (sic).'

What *he*, Baudelaire, expresses deliciously is:

O mystical metamorphosis
Of all my senses melted to one!
(*The Flowers of Evil*)

And from this disrespectful parallel between Symbolists and molluscs flows, for Max Nordau, an obvious physiological likeness. Poetic impressionism, he concludes, 'brings human thinking back to its zoological beginnings, as artistic activity, in its current state of high sensory differentiation, is reduced to an embryonic form in which all the arts, which later would diverge, were still confused, pell-mell; and undeveloped ...'[44] Elsewhere:

Bringing back the loaded word of ideas to the emotional sound, is to renounce all the results of organic evolution, and to belittle man, happy in possession of language, to the rank of the rustling cricket, or the frog that croaks [...]

'It is to downgrade us to the beginnings of organic development. It's a falling away, from the height of human perfection to the low level of the clam, and to proclaim as progress the return of the human consciousness to that of an oyster.'[45]

So, this atavistic return is precisely for Mr Max Nordau a 'peculiarity of degeneration.' Here he is fixated on the Symbolists and the 'case of Wagner,' as Nietzsche put it; once again, he can claim prophetically—a degeneration of degenerations; that everything is degeneration! ...

We must ask ourselves then, what answers the impartial review of acquired facts—on the one hand – and notions of evolutionary biology—on the other.

First of all, it doesn't seem that the observers have been struck by the morbid nature of the effects of synaesthesia. Dr Breton notes Auditory-colouration in a '24-year-old woman, who was otherwise healthy, intelligent, without underlying conditions.'[46] 'In the various observations we will report,' says Destouches,[47] 'the neuropathic state of the subjects has been carefully noted. All, or almost all, have no anomalies, either in the visual apparatus or with respect to mental ideation.' The sensibility of colouration has, thus far, been researched as a hysterical reaction, 'but could it naturally exist outside of any pathological state? We are convinced of this'—replies Dr Le Dantec— 'though without being able to provide convincing proof of our assertion.'[48]

Admittedly, it is possible to observe these phenomena coinciding with proven decline: 'A patient of Legrain attached a connection between improvement in his illness by distinctions in a sense of colour, from black to white ...'[49] 'And it is certain that this faculty gains notably in vivacity at moments of fatigue, nervousness, or high emotion ...'—'It goes without saying,' writes Flournoy, 'to conclude from this that the pathological nature of Auditory-colouration has the same basis as the treatment of memory or the association of Ideas pertaining to Morbid Phenomena, because they are often excited or exacerbated by the delirium of fever or insanity.'[50]

Hashish can also bring about these sensations, extemporaneously. But the sensation under the influence of hashish is not degeneration, for it is 'contained.'

Finally, it does not seem that a particularly refined brain is required for synaesthesia to occur, nor a delicate mechanism inclined to morbidity. There is no exclusion of those with a conservative equanimity, the middle class of mental faculties. Lemaître, whose investigation focuses on four classes at the Geneva College, finds them 'more frequent than might be supposed' in boys aged 13 to 14. He does not seem to have noticed among them many child prodigies. Sensory correlation can be the preserve of the simple or the mediocre, stripping this term of its usual pejorative sense.

It is, in the end, quite illusory and artificial to attempt to include, under the same indulgent or pitiless rubric, such a heterogeneity of phenomena. Any normal and healthy synaesthesia from the intellectual sphere (category A), may, within the same individual, become symptomatic of a mental disorder if it turns into hallucination or obsession (category B). It's a question of degree, of mere measurement. So that, from one synaesthesia to another, the diagnostic conclusion, the morbid equivalence, can vary considerably. If we affirm

Auditory-colouration to be compatible with the healthiest mentality, the reciprocal, at least in the externalised state, is more disturbing: Illusions and visual hallucinations are relatively benign. Auditory hallucinations, however, can herald serious troubles. Still, we should recognise that they are, among the synaesthesia, a reassuring rarity.

This is the *clinical* and statistical argument that we must, first of all, pose to Max Nordau. As he has brought the question into the field of eminent biology we will follow him there.

'Natural development always goes from Unity to Diversity,' he says, 'not backwards. Progress consists of the *differentiation* and not the reconglomeration of differentiated beings; of a rich originality rather than an archaic agar without physiognomy ...'[51]

Max Nordau seems to have confused the *sensory chaos* which preceded the development of perception with the *synthetic tendency* that is the current culmination of it. Certainly, before this synthesis was attempted, it was necessary to have become aware of its elements. Now, having speciated them, one may merge them again, no longer, this time, into a chaotic jumble – not this 'agar without physiognomy' of which he speaks, but of a *conscious order*, without regressive restrictions, nor need we assume one must be reduced to the state of mind of a mollusc, even to be the possessor of the famous siphon. Sensory correlations have, in the complexity of their nature, a degree of morbidity. But, in their essence, they seem to us, we reaffirm, normal, and suitable for the eternal Procession of Ideas, this great law which succeeds chaos with Analysis, analysis with Synthesis.

Such is the formula of any science: Physics and Chemistry were at first only Metaphysics and Alchemy, dark globules of general systems ... then Analysis illuminated the march: the great triad of Scheele, Lavoisier and Priestley began the differentiation of the elements, which, in our day, have come together to remake the unifying nature of modern chemistry, through which the forces reveal their equivalences and their infinite transmutations (see Jouve, Maxwell). All this is progress, certainly, and has nothing in common with those naïve dissertations set out by the first physicians or the old Hermetics.

Finally this is the stage of the current philosophical movement: To pass from the 'same to the other,' (Hegel) to relay, by a rational dialectic, the diversities of the sensible world, thus approaching the last term of the knowledge, which must be a *coherent Heterogeneity* (Herbert Spencer).

Moreover, followed to the end, Max Nordau's arguments would tend to convict Classical antiquity itself of the worst degenerations. This fact would make it difficult to remain respectful of the Hellenic traditions, for they have bequeathed these traditions to us in the form of a natural and fatal strategy, the *Belles-lettres*; that imposing cohort of 'Figures of Speech' piously organised and labelled by rhetoricians and didactics.

The analogous use of synaesthesia, as a means to occasionally animate and illuminate the often cold and clammy mechanism known as 'the style,' seems to us to be a justified one. It is a new Trope, not considered by the early grammarians, but made possible by the progressive refinement of sensory acuity. We would gladly seat them beneath the grammatical epithet of our time -*synaesthesia*—at the sharp end of allegory, in the neighbourhood of metonymy.

The grammatic parallel is easy to pursue. The Trope, a 'Figure of Synaesthesia,' can be defined as: 'A more lively way of speaking, intended either to make the idea sensible by means of an image, a comparison, or to be further refined and attuned to its perspective; to its atavism.' This, in terms of rhetoric, is a perfectly orthodox definition.

Now, having concluded in favour of the beauty and figural reality of synaesthesia, it may be piquant to appropriate Mr Max Nordau's aggressive methods in relation to sensory correlations, held so dear by the Symbolists and decadents; to extend these methods, directly to the honoured Greco-Latin figures of speech; to thus show, in each of their terms, how there corresponds in mental pathology, a morbid lacuna, a defect, a symptom of decay; to draw up, beside the pompous list inherited from the archaic grammarians, a symmetrical list of their *Morbid Equivalents*.

A demonstration of the absurd can sometimes have its benefit. We would say then: At the *Prosopopoeia*, at the *Apostrophe*, by which those absent, those inanimate, those dead are brought to life, to respond, in the world of 'Ill-Ideas,' to *visual* and *auditory hallucinations*, 'personifications of all sorts.'

The *Onomatopoeia* is of no less significance atavistically. The regression is flagrant: 'The onomatopoeia is the beginning of both speech and hieroglyphic writing,' says Fée (Larousse). The voices of a whole menagerie of animals were expressed in Latin[52] by distinctive Onomatopoeia, which we are now unaware of. It is no more the phoneticism of an oyster that we echo, Mr Nordau might this time note, since the receptor-siphon already decried is incapable of making sounds, but to the psychology of the 'creaky cricket' or the 'frog which ribbits' it isn't much more reassuring. Virgil did not understand what atavistic retrocession he was illustrating when he wrote:

Quadrupedante putrem sonitu quatit ungula campum.[53]

Besides, the *Aeneid* would contain, at this rate, many other stigmas:

Obsessions and *fixated Ideas* often have, for pretext, the figure of speech known as 'Repetition':

Me, me, adsum qui feci ... [54]

The pathogenic germ came from elsewhere; Cicero:

Who is the author of this law?—Rullus. Who deprived the majority of the Roman people of their votes?—Rullus.—Who chaired the comitia? Rullus.

The amnesias are flagrant, under the cover of reticence:

Quos ego ... [55]

roared Neptune, and, not finding the term, cautiously switched the topic of conversation.

Demosthenes, haranguing corpses—the Greek dead at Marathon—Socrates, through the mouth of Plato invoking the Laws—Cicero challenging the Republic (*1st Catiline*)—Lucan portraying the Motherland as a weeping woman with flowing hair (the *Pharsalia*), each have thus made use of the deranged, the hysterical and insane. These are the twin follies: and so we have the 'Prosopopoeia of two,' the *Dialogism*.

The *Metaphor*, in which the word is diverted from its primitive sense, perfectly simulates certain *Paraphasias*. 'What is this object?' we ask, for example, by pointing out a glass to a patient in Dr Pitres's department. 'It is a lock,' replies the poor man, with confidence, who, in the heroic days of oratory, would have been taxed only for use of excessive metaphors. But in the confines of the clinic, he is a paraphasic: Truth lies this side of the hospital gates ...

Yet metaphor is 'one of the most powerful instruments of human language,' says Max Müller.—'The Metaphor was the characteristic feature of a whole period in the primitive history of language, the *mythical period*,' with a homonymic tendency, where the roots were few and each possessed many meanings. These few roots with multiple meanings correspond, it seems to us, to the clam's siphon, a siphon singular and yet 'numerous.' And Mr Max Nordau himself wouldn't hesitate to bring this mythical period out of this stage of sensory evolution which he calls 'gelatinous.' So then, is the use of metaphor in our era of multiple and differentiated vocabulary to be regarded as regressive and *degenerate*? Either way, it is impossible to be purified: 'Under the microscope of Etymology, almost every word reveals traces of its first metaphorical conception.'[56]

So, no more talk? ... No further thought? ... What would Mr Max Nordau proscribe to this timorous surrender?

§

Still imperturbable, forceful in its sincerity, the Figure of Synaesthesia continues on its march and marks a stage in literature. This Synaesthetic-Sensation specifies the time of our sensory evolution. Still scattered and rebellious to the mind, yet already numerous are those who can testify; they seem still to be in progress; coordinates, located like tracings along the new functions of mentality.

Without auguring for an as-yet unimagined fruition, we do believe the ground to be fertile for future aesthetic pleasures. On this, Mr Saint-Pol-Roux tells us 'You see, the maximizing of art in literature might only be acquired by a contingency of all the federated senses which are finally controlled by what I once called the 'Vatican of sensation,' that is to say, the mind.—Yes, the senses, bunched, are crushed in the mental press and thereby exacted; the fortified wine of expression ... The art becomes complete, *synthetic, symphonic.*'

Having unified our feelings we can expand the field. For in the infinite scale of vibratory movement, only some modalities are material; again, there's further joy here for the senses. We can extend them—no longer need we be contented with the seven colours of the spectrum,[57] the seven degrees of diatonicism ... We have rendered the ultraviolet rays detectable by relaxing the accidentals in archaic ranges. Let's go beyond. We are bathed by a sea of unknown ripples, of which each rhythm, each period is perhaps an artistic element, a 'latent source of enjoyment. Let's surprise them, violate nature, if need be, it is our right.'[58] Thus, the Chimera fluttered around the impassive Sphinx, eager and curious:

> I am looking for new perfumes, wider flowers and untested pleasures.[59]

But the Sphinx, for a long time, remained imperturbable; motionless and mute.

VICTOR SEGALEN

Notes

1   The term (*les Synesthésies*) is that of Jules Millet. It is equivalent to the expression "associated sensations". Auditory-colouration (*l'Audition colorée*) is a particular case in point.

2   Dr Louis Destouches: *Music and some of its Sensory Effects*. Theses, Paris, 1898.

3   J. Combarieu: *The reports of music and poetry from the point of view of expression*, 1893.

4   Read from right to left: Iod-Hé-Vau-Hè. IEVE and not IAVE. But any literal translation is inaccurate, because the phonetics of Hebrew do not actually contain vowels, but "aspirations".

5   *The Initiation*, August 1901: "Sun, light, colour in the stars."

6   *Annals of Oculistics*, Dr Dujardin, Lille. January 1898.

7*   This is the title Segalen has, presumably for emphasis, applied to the book; Goethe's was merely *Of Colour Theory* (*Zur Farbenlehre*).

8   Destouches: *op. cit.*, pp. 16, 17, 18.

9   J.-K. Huysmans: *À Rebours*, p. 63.

10   Aug. Lemaître: *Auditory-colouration and related phenomena observed in schoolchildren*. In *Rev. Scientifique*, 16th February, 1901.

11   Destouches, *op. cit.*

12   It's unnecessary to insist on the impossibility of our machine to think practically toward attaining this theoretical stage. Abstraction is always tainted with some motion of the senses. It remembers some old believer

whose brain, fed by scholasticism, was, it affirms, sufficiently trained towards pure Idea, particularly towards Trinitarian Abstraction, to conceive it without figures, to conceive it without symbols. Alas! In the days of more minute analysis, the good theologian confesses that the mystery of the Trinity he saw was a violet colour; the sensations have resumed their rights. -So for the Moral. 'Pure Idea is always more or less contaminated by personal interests—of Caste, or of Party, and the word 'justice,' for example, takes on all kinds of specialized and limited meanings under which its supreme sense is crushed and disappears.' (R. de Gourmont: 'Words and Ideas', *Mercury*, January 1900, pp. 23-24.)

13   Rimbaud had, at 18, published *The Drunken Boat*. At 20, *The Illuminations*. V. Hugo had said 'he is Shakespeare's child.' Then abruptly, the poet in him disappeared to make way for the explorer. Across Ethiopia an echo came to him from the sound of his works: he took no notice of it, and conscientiously abdicated all literary prestige.

14   G. Kahn, *Revue Bleue*, 10th August, 1901.

15   Destouches: *op. cit.*, pp. 8-10.

16   L. Favre: *Music of the Colours*.

17   The German word 'Klangfarbe' corresponds precisely in meaning with 'timbre', that is to say 'sound-colour'.

18   Alfred Binet: *The Problem of coloured hearing*. In *Revue des Deux-Mondes*, 1892, 1st October.

19   *Ibid.*

20   *Cloches en la nuit*, 1889.

21*   Nicolas Boileau-Despréaux (1636–1711) is here likened to the over-arching presence of Notre Dame, to which he retreated in 1705, and from where he wrote his clerically-supressed 12th and final Satire.

22   *The Restoration of the Procession*, Saint-Pol-Roux, 1893.

23   'Behold the city of Marseilles, in whose walls I was born, and of which, after more than twenty years of partial absence, I still spill the bright gold seed from my veins of ink, because this art, that no pale shade would reproach me for, is, in fact, the apotheosis of natural joy and human energies.' (*The Restoration of the Procession*)

24   *Lady of the Faulx*, Saint-Pol-Roux, 1893.

25   *The Restoration of the Procession*: Roscanvel.

26   *'The shrill sound of the trumpet'*

27   'I was then in my sixteenth year,' wrote Wagner 'during the day, in a half-sleep, I had visions, in which the Fundamental, the Third, the Fifth appeared to me in person, and revealed to me their important meaning.' *My Life*, 1870.

28   Destouches, *op. cit.* p. 4.

29   Engel: *Stumpf*, quoted by Destouches, *ibid*.

30   *En Route*. Stock, 1899, pp. 5-15.

31   *Lakmé*, act III.

32*   All examples are of Wagnerian operas, composed 1854-82.

33   "The word," says Remy de Gourmont, "still has a shape determined by the consonants: a perfume, but hardly perceived, given the infirmity of our imaginative senses."

34   *The Rose and the Thorns of the Road*: Ideoplasty.

35*   J.-K. Huysmans: *À Rebours*, Charpentier, 1899, p. 64. The current essay was Segalen's second paper published in 1902, his first, *Medical Observations Regarding Naturalist*

Writers, Y. Cadoret, 1902, largely consisted of a series of mental diagnoses of fictional literary characters, focussing on the figure he mentions here—Jean Des Esseintes, protagonist of J.-K. Huysmans' novel *À Rebours* (translated as both *Against the Grain* and *Against Nature*). As a recluse, keeping to his house with his sensual experiences as almost his sole purpose, Des Esseintes prefigures the antagonist of *In a Sound World*.

36   *The Rose and the Thorns of the Road*: the Gluttonous Eye, p. 209.

37   Dr Dantec, professor at the School of Naval Health of Bordeaux. *Archives of Naval Medicine*, 1893, p. 95.

38   Remy de Gourmont: *Orisons of Evil*.

39   *Intern. congress of. Psychol.*, 1892, quoted by Destouches, *op. cit*.

40   Destouches, *op. cit.*, p. 56.

41   On this subject we must thank our friends the sublime poets George Varenne and Pierre Richard for making available to us their musical application of these theories through conforming the rhythms and the sonorities in their 'Coloured Songs'.

42   This is not a peculiar property to this mollusc, as the first amoeba can testify. The Pholade, or angel-wing clam, is especially known to zoologists for more curious properties: among them, it emits light by the interaction of two ferments.

43   Max Nordau: *Degeneration*, Volume I. *Les Symbolistes*, pp. 245-255.

44   M. Nordau, op. cit., Volume II, p. 430

45   *Ibid.*, Volume I, pp. 245-255.

46   *Journal of Practitioners*, 1st May, 1897.

47   Destouches, *op. cit.*, p. 16.

48   *Arch. Med. Nav.*, 1893, p. 95.

49   Legrain, quoted by Max Nordau, in *Degeneration*, t. I.

50   Destouches, *op. cit.*, p. 26.

51   M. Nordau: *Degeneration* t. I. p. 313. Thus spoke Jehovah 'Creator and sovereign Lord' when, after the fall, he granted the archangel Zachariel 'Prince of Earth's Dominions' (here probably symbolizing the fatal mechanism of heredity) the mission to govern the created forms: 'so that no order of its matrix should fail to conform to its generators. You will maintain the species, so that one does not encroach on the other. Watch over the kingdoms, destroy the *primordial mother jelly* common to both what lives and moves and what lives and does not move. Hold that the plant does not eat, that the animal does not bloom, that at the bottom of the sea there shall not grow disturbing gems, nor dubious creatures. That all eyes are endowed with sight, that each organ has a unique role ... That the antennas which listen are not those that are used for smell, and if tiny animals raise forests beneath the ocean waves, that their work be annihilated, for I am the creator and nothing will have either essence nor form that is not borne of my hand ...' Remy de Gourmont: *Lilith*. This was the stage necessary for differentialism, though only the beginnings of sensory evolution.

52   And more in Annamite or Chinese (Dr Louis Laurent).

53   *'The four-footed galloping sound of hooves shakes the plain'* (Virgil)

54   *'Me, me here, it was I'* (Virgil).

55   *'Whom I ...'* (Virgil) an example of aposiopesis, whereby a sentence is left ...

56   Max Müller.

57   Moreau (de Tours) commenting on Jules Millet.

58   *Ibid.*

59   Flaubert: *The Temptation of St. Anthony*.

* Translator's footnote.

Resonance, difference, dismemberment

Victor Segalen's
Dans Un Monde Sonore

David Toop

Humans, maybe certain predominant types of human, perceive the world and its plausible reality as clustering masses, things, objects, fixity, spaces and solids to be seen, touched and tasted, all existing in uneasy relationship to a less stable, semi-verifiable world of intangibles, the domains of time, mind, feeling, air, scent, sound and other mysteries. At levels deeper than surface appearances materiality is far less constant and stable than it seems but humans derive comfort from some degree of solidity. As Jane Bennett writes in *Vibrant Matter*: "'Objects' appear as such because their becoming proceeds at a speed or a level below the threshold of human discernment. It is hard indeed to keep one's mind wrapped around a materiality that is not reducible to extension in space, difficult to dwell with the notion of an incorporeality or a differential of intensities. This is because to live, humans need to interpret the world reductively as a series of fixed objects, a need reflected in the rhetorical role assigned to the word *material*. As noun or adjective *material* denotes some stable or rock-bottom reality, something adamantine."[1]

Imagine then a reverse world in which reality is imagined or designed as a vaporous flux of vibration and resonance, in which words dissolve into shimmering echoes, physicality becomes diffuse, almost lost in a dream state of aurality. Within sight of Java during a return journey from Tahiti to France, this was what Victor Segalen began to envision in 1904. In a note to himself, an admonition to begin a book on exoticism, he wrote: "Study each of the senses and its relation to exoticism: sight, the sky. Hearing: exotic melodies. Smell above all. No taste or touch."[2] The book was never finished though in its incomplete state, *Essay on Exoticism: An Aesthetics of Diversity* was published in 1955, long after Segalen's death. The project of smell was also unfulfilled but Segalen did write a short novel on hearing as an experimental, primary sense. *Dans Un Monde Sonore* was published in August 1907, by Mercure de France. This perplexing little book could be considered a companion volume to *Voix Mortes: Musiques Maories*, an ethnomusicological text dedicated to his friend Claude Debussy and published in October of the same year. Both are significant markers in historical sound studies; thus far they are not recognised as such.

Victor   Segalen—doctor,   archaeologist,   writer, ethnographer, musician, sinologist, traveller—was born in Brest in 1878. As a medical student he wrote his thesis on neurotics in contemporary literature, situating himself in a productive convergence of science and art that bears comparison with Freud's placement of Egyptian funerary figures within his line of sight as he listened to analysands. Presumably for research Segalen met Max Nordau, a social critic violently opposed to decadents, Symbolists, mystics, Pre-Raphaelites and other so-called degenerates of the *fin de siècle*; Joris-Karl Huysmans, whose *À Rebours* was the quintessential novel of nineteenth century neurosis and all that Nordau disdained, and Remy de Gourmont, a Symbolist writer associated with Mercure de France, hence Segalen's first conduit to a publisher.

Of equal or greater importance was his meeting with Claude Debussy in April 1906. Segalen was an active, *physical* traveller, already having sailed to Tahiti, where he sought out traces of Gauguin, and Djibouti, where he investigated the fainter trail of Rimbaud. Later he lived for five years in China. Debussy, on the other hand, barely travelled at all, other than for professional engagements, musical excursions and reluctant family holidays. "When you lack the means to travel," he once wrote, "you must find compensation in your fantasy." Yet the two of them connected through a shared fascination with atmospheres and resonance. In 1889 Debussy had heard Vietnamese (Annamite) theatre music and Javanese gamelan at the Paris Exposition Universelle, a celebration of both French colonial power and the centenary of the beginning of the French revolution. What he heard left a deep impression, strong enough to linger through his life and in some mysterious, arguably tenuous way permeate aspects of his composing, particularly piano works such as *Pagodes*, *Et la lune descend sur le temple qui fut*, *Cloches à travers les feuilles* and *Reflets dans l'eau*.

More pertinent than these speculations on influence is Debussy's endorsement of musical cultures more commonly considered unworthy of comment or regard. In effect, though his ghost may not agree, he expressed admiration for the music of peoples who were generally treated as a sub-human species. As the Argentinian ethnomusicologist Ramón Pelinski wrote: "Debussy's interest in Far-Eastern music was no *nostalgie du pittoresque à bon marché* such as we often find among the orientalizing composers of the nineteenth century. To him must be credited the insight that extra-European music can stand in complete accord with his own aims as a composer ... Extra-European man and his music is thus placed on an entirely equal footing."[3] Broadly speaking, this was compatible with Segalen's anti-exotic version of exoticism, in which Polynesian music, Hindu philosophy and Chinese paintings were all treated with great seriousness as exemplars of diversity. In one of the transcriptions he made of conversations between himself and Debussy, Segalen wrote: "One of Debussy's preoccupations is with the inadequacy of the percussion section. Note: bring back from my Far Eastern trip a set of gongs and cymbals."

Debussy biographer Stephen Walsh suggests that Segalen's appearance in his life may have rekindled the composer's enthusiasm for Asian music, though the initial motive was to persuade Debussy into a collaboration, an opera based on the life of the Buddha. Debussy felt there was little he could do with the subject; instead he proposed something of mutually agreeable interest based on the Orpheus myth. As Debussy said to Segalen: "Orpheus was not a man, nor any human being, living or dead. Orpheus is the Desire to hear and be heard. Orpheus is the symbol of Power in the world of sound."[4]

For Vladimir Jankélévitch, Debussy was one of a small group of composers who gave voice to the songs of Orpheus, thereby underlining music's role as a humanising, civilising force. "Music is not simply a captivating and fallacious ruse," he wrote in *Music and the Ineffable*, "subjugating without violence, capturing by captivating; it is also gentleness that makes gentle: in itself gentle, it makes those who hear it more gentle since music pacifies the monsters of instinct in all of us and tames passion's wild animals."[5] This notion of 'taming' is central to the Orpheus myth. With his lyre he healed and divined, charmed animals, ghosts, even stones (what language does a stone speak?). The myth is shamanic, even more so when Orpheus is torn apart, dismembered body scattered in the river, his decapitated head and lyre continuing to emanate music as they float downstream. J.W. Waterhouse painted one version of the scene in 1900, the pubescent nymphs so typical of his oeuvre gazing wistfully down at a handsome Pre-Raphaelite head framed not at all grotesquely by flowing hair. Odilon Redon created a number of far stranger versions: one, circa 1881, in which the singing head sits on the lyre, passenger on an improvised boat; another, drawn in pastels between 1903 and 1910, in which head and lyre are conjoined into one portative, man-machine instrument, its song ecstatically fusing with water and sky. "A final detail of the Orpheus myth is clearly shamanic," Mircea Eliade wrote in *Shamanism: Archaic Techniques of Ecstasy*. "Cut off by the bacchantes and thrown into the Hebrus, Orpheus's head floated to Lesbos, singing. It later served as an oracle, like the head of Mimir. Now the skulls of the Yukagir shamans also play a role in divination."[6]

The Orpheus project came nowhere near completion. Segalen remained poignantly hopeful but Debussy prevaricated. He was critical of Segalen's libretto—"More literary than lyrical"—and moved on to a new obsession, the possibility of an opera based on Edgar Allan Poe's *The Fall of the House of Usher*. Segalen also moved on. There is confusion over the timeline but at some point during these fruitless discussions he wrote and published *Dans Un Monde Sonore*. Coincidentally or not, the opening paragraphs are reminiscent of Poe's story. A narrator approaches an isolated house in order to revive an old acquaintance. In both cases there is a woman in the house and the men that the narrators meet both suffer from what Poe describes as "a morbid acuteness of the senses"; Roderick Usher has developed an intolerance of all but the most insipid sense impressions, though he can listen to "peculiar sounds" from stringed instruments.

André, Segalen's equivalent of Usher, is described as harmlessly mad, though the way he has chosen to live is radically disconcerting. As Monsieur Leurais discovers, the room to which his old friend has retreated is so prominently resonant that his account of collecting sensory data from indigenous Papuans in the Straits of Torres is transformed as if passed "through a harmonizing orchestra." Even this constant droning effect is insufficient for André's hypersensitive, 'adjusted' hearing. He intensifies the effect to create a prolongation of spoken syllables, a "bush of whispers", buzzing echoes and delays. The scene anticipates by more than sixty years Alvin Lucier's *I am Sitting in a Room*, in which a spoken text become unintelligible as resonant frequencies within the room gradually blur the sense of its words, but it also responds to the synaesthetic effect of Stéphane Mallarmé's poetry, in which words and their music saturate the properties of the other. "Music of colour, music of words—such were the slogans of the day," wrote Debussy biographer Edward Lockspeiser.[7] In a 'theoretical fiction' entitled *Mallarmé's Nose*, Allen S. Weiss describes the *fin de siècle* obsession with perceptual transferences as a delirium of potential, an intoxication in which all that is solid melts into air: "Mallarmé now knew that not only did the world exist to be transformed into a book, but that the book could also exist to be transfigured into a perfume! *Per fumum*, through smoke! Poetic alchemy. He would sublimate *L'Après-Midi d'un Faune* into perfume!"[8]

A similar delirium has infected André: the desire to live within sound; to defy the tyranny of sight. Harps and resonating cylinders line his room; two singing flames flicker in glass tubes, closely tuned to produce beat frequencies. There is a banality to it, pure physics, Leurais realises, as the apparatus of the installation reveals itself from within the mist of sound. Segalen was clearly aware of nineteenth century experiments in acoustics. Similar devices can be found in Hermann von Helmholtz's pioneering study, *On the Sensations of Tone*, first published in Germany in 1863. Among its contents were sections on resonators (illustrated by drawings of globular and bottle shaped resonating vessels), the mechanics of sympathetic resonance, combinational tones and beats, the composition of vibrations and the musical tones of strings. Closer to Segalen's lifetime was John Tyndall's *Sound*, published in 1867, though Tyndall noted that learned Germans were more understanding of his intentions than a reviewer of the French translation. Based on a series of lectures designed to make the science of sound and acoustics comprehensible and interesting "to all intelligent persons, including those who do not possess any special scientific culture," Tyndall's book has an experimental vitality to it. Easy to imagine these demonstrations—strings excited by tuning forks, musical sounds produced by holding a card against the toothed wheel of a gyroscope, smoke columns responding to the sounds of a voice or cough, sound from water vapour and flames bursting spontaneously into song—slipping into the realm of magic, opium hallucination, theatrical illusion, the bizarre sonic instruments described in Raymond Roussel's *Locus Solus* and *Impressions of Africa* and, in the twenty-first century, sound art installations.

As James Kennaway demonstrates in his book, *Bad Medicine: The History of the Idea of Music as a Cause of Disease*, ideas of degenerate culture, neurasthenia, pathological music and the composer as 'mad genius' took root in the late nineteenth century. Writers like Nordau, consulted by Segalen, attributed musical degeneracy to the growing effects of modernity and the 'over-excitement'

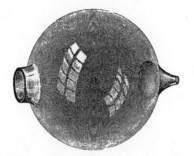

1. Hollow glass sphere resonators used by Hermann Helmholtz (published in *On the Sensations of Tone*) to identify tones by sympathetic resonance. The spheres have two openings, one sharp edged, the other funnel shaped. The funnel shaped opening fits into the ear, secured and made airtight by sealing wax. The other ear is stopped by a plug of wax. The effect is to muffle tones in the surrounding air, other than the tone of the resonator. This tone, according to Helmholtz, "brays into the ear most powerfully."

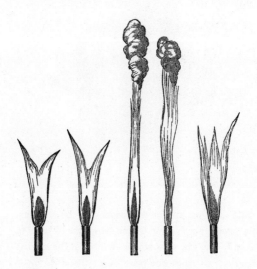

2. Experiment by John Tyndall (published in *Sound*, 1867) in which flames from circular apertures were lengthened or shortened by sonorous vibrations. A shrill whistle blown close to the flames caused the flames to react differently, according to the nature of the flames. The long flames became short, forked and brilliant whereas the short flames became long and smoky.

of two wars. More sinister consequences followed in the wake of such beliefs. "The theory of degeneration," writes Kennaway, "provided not only a framework for viewing certain music as not only a symptom but also as a means of bringing out latent degeneration in listeners, just as it might bring out latent homosexuality or damage already vulnerable nerves ... the discourse of pathological music was to be radicalized and racialized in the early decades of the twentieth century, making it overtly political and dangerous ..."[9]

There is also a pathological element to shamanism, the catastrophic onset of sickness which resolves into shamanistic practice, expressed through metaphors of dismemberment. The body is torn apart, then reconfigured to function beyond the material world. Imagine Orpheus playing music to stones, surely a form of degeneracy according to Nordau. Orpheus also descends into the underworld in the hope of saving his wife Eurydice from death. "The shaman specializes in a trance during which his soul is believed to leave his body and ascend to the sky or descend to the underworld," Eliade writes in *Shamanism*.[10] By living within sound André both disembodies himself (the signs of change are evident in his face, its "blind gesture" and unnaturally active ears) and plunges himself into an echoing underworld of resonance and vibration. His wife, Mathilde, is lost to him because she refuses to relinquish sight as her primary sense. "She can not hear in the dark," he laments. Darkness is the domain of the listener. Segalen overturns received ideas about the seductive degeneracy of sound, making sight the perverted, reverted sense, the primitive sense of sharpened sight that allowed prehistoric humans to tear apart their prey.

At this point of loss in *Dans Un Monde Sonore*, the Orpheus myth is made explicit by Leurais in his narration: "I readily imagine Orpheus, the singer of hymns, abandoning the world of a thousand lyres, and descending to the infernal caves—by which one can take to symbolise exactly the brute material world, mute and deaf, this is the most ignoble and truest of all Myths that men have configured." Echoing Debussy's words, that Orpheus is not a human being, living or dead, Orpheus is understood as an allegory whose apogee was to enable a vision of what it might be to live in sound. Base materiality dissolves in this imagined world, but then so does music (a process begun by Debussy, as much as any other, through his explorations of the resonant interior of the piano).

Segalen's narrator asks the question: what is the true world? Perhaps he was aware of Hermann von Helmholtz's insight into the inferential nature of the senses and their role in creating our sense of reality. "In reviewing the received hegemony of the senses and suggesting the possibility of other configurations," writes Charles Forsdick, "Segalen reveals a vigorous awareness of the role of visual/textual bias within the construction of Western knowledge and suggests that consciousness of this is a new way not only of sensing other worlds, but also, more fundamentally, of making sense of others."[11]

"Two creatures stand facing each other, muzzle to muzzle," Segalen wrote in *Equipée*, "arguing over a coin from some indecipherable reign. The creature on the left

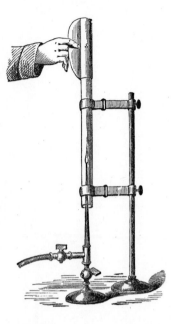

3. Experiment by John Tyndall in which a gas flame enclosed within a tube produces an audible tone. A paper slider was used to lengthen and shorten the tube, demonstrating that if the slider was raised then the pitch would instantly fall and if lowered then the pitch would rise.

is a dragon, trembling and not all twisted up on itself in decadent Chinese coils, but with short wings and scales that vibrate all the way down to the tips of its claws. This is the imagination in its most understated style. The creature on the right is a broad, supple, arched tiger, muscled and taut and powerfully sexual: the Real, always so sure of itself."[12] There is no question of which creature ultimately triumphs within the essentially bourgeois household of André and Mathilde. "I could have strangled the both of them," says Leurais at the end of his story.

Writing of Segalen's first book, *Les Immémoriaux*, anthropologist James Clifford speaks of his rendering of the doomed tradition of Polynesia as a sonorous world, an

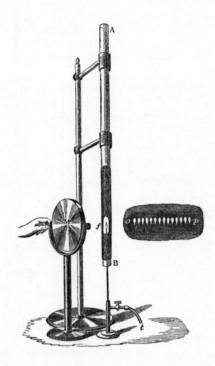

4. Experiment by John Tyndall, showing a gas flame burning in a glass tube. The back of the tube was blackened. A concave mirror was placed in front of the flame. This mirror was then turned by Tyndall. "Were the flame silent and steady," he wrote, "we should obtain a *continuous* band of light; but it quivers, and emits at the same time a deep note." As he turned the mirror quickly, the luminous chain of images was drawn more widely apart; as he turned it slowly, they closed up, "the chain of flames passing through the most beautiful variations."

environment of spoken and heard intimacies. In *Voix Mortes*, Segalen quoted from the words of another traveller—Max Radiguet's *Les Derniers Sauvages*, published in 1860: "A sort of grumbling murmur was heard; amazing sensual sniffing answered him: then there were small hoarse clamours, good humoured and satisfied ... guttural sighs, caressing complaints, pushed out of arid throats ... raucous flames and unexpected accents again ... for a moment the tumult subsided, and only breaths were heard, breathless."[13]

"Moreover," wrote Clifford, "the sonorous world of *Les Immémoriaux* is associated with an inevitable cultural death. In China Segalen moved away from this style of cultural evocation, but he felt a constant nostalgia for the sensuous absorption associated with sound. His last, fragmentary poems were a series of long-lined odes—*Thibet* (he clung to the aspirated spelling)—songs of the most exotic place, a pure, transcendent echochamber. Segalen never reached Tibet, the ultimate, deferred goal of all his expeditions."[14] Instead, in May 1919 he was found dead at the age of forty-one, collapsed in woods near his birthplace, a deep gash in his ankle and an open copy of *Hamlet* by his side. "From the very heart of the matter," he wrote in June 1908, "I imagined that things were speaking."[15] They continue to speak, yet their sense is partially lost in buzzing, echoes, resonance, a forest of whispers.

Notes

1   Bennett, Jane, *Vibrant Matter: a political ecology of things*, Duke University Press, 2010, p. 58.

2   Segalen, Victor, *Essay On Exoticism*, translated by Yaël Rachel Schlick, Duke University Press, 2002, p. 13.

3   Pelinski, Ramón, *Musical Exoticism around the year 1900: Claude Debussy*, published in *World Cultures and Modern Art*, Bruckmann Publishers, 1972, p. 235.

4   Walsh, Stephen, *Debussy: A Painter In Sound*, Faber & Faber, 2018, p. 197.

5   Jankélévitch, Vladimir, *Music and the Ineffable*, translated by Carolyn Abbate, Princeton University Press, 2003, p. 4.

6   Eliade, Mircea, *Shamanism: Archaic Techniques of Ecstasy*, Routledge and Kegan Paul, 1970, p. 391.

7   Lockspeiser, Edward, *Debussy*, J.M. Dent & Sons, 1963, p. 39.

8   Weiss, Allen S., *Mallarmé's Nose*, published in *HEAT* no. 13, 1999, p. 113.

9   Kennaway, James, *Bad Vibrations*, Ashgate, 2012, pp. 94-97.

10   Eliade, Mircea, *op. cit.*, p. 5.

11   Forsdick, Charles, *Sight, Sound, and Synaesthesia: Reading the Senses in Victor Segalen*, published in *Sensual Reading: New Approaches to Reading in its Relation to the Senses*, ed. Michael Syrotinski and Ian Maclachan, Bucknell University Press, 2001, p. 242.

12   Segalen, Victor, *Journey To the Land of the Real*, a translation of *Equipée* by Natasha Lehrer, Atlas Press, 2016, p. 128.

13   Segalen, Victor, *Voix Mortes: Musiques Maories*, Éditions Novetlé, 1995, pp. 19-20.

14   Clifford, James, *The Predicament of Culture*, Harvard University Press, 1988, p. 155.

15   Segalen, Victor, *Essay On Exoticism*, *op. cit.*, p. 13.

Textual Notes

Orpheus Rex

Three years, Debussy discussed this opera with Segalen; was it ever to be? In his memoirs, Debussy's friend, Louis Laloy recounted, "A little later, we made the acquaintance of Victor Segalen, whose intellectual research was interesting but as far as could be from any music, especially that of Debussy. Since he was very cordial, however, my friend dared not upset him and lost much time discussing the text of *Orpheus Rex* with him, continually correcting and reworking it. After Segalen's premature death, the drama was published under the care of his widow, and I would be remiss if I were to cause offence by being overly zealous, but without diminishing the merit of the writer, it must be recognized that he posed to the musician a problem, or rather, an insolvable enigma."

No, for all that, there wasn't to be any music. But there should have been! Not by Debussy, whose ethereal eliding and folding of certainty only allowed for a single and singular opera. On reading *Orphée-Roi* I found myself burbling in the turgid sludge and shrills of a full rococo melodrama; Rameau perhaps, later Berlioz or Wagner, whom Segalen was elsewhere preoccupied with. From among the composers who, like

Debussy, struggled against the spectre of Opera, Beethoven and Liszt might have had the unremitting force and cussed nature to work it through, empathetic to the character of such a disaffected tale.

Liszt wrote a symphonic poem entitled Orpheus whilst conducting Gluck's famous opera of the subject, which he quietly exchanged for the overture as if it were a part of the work; Berlioz also had a tinker with it.

But *Orpheus* has a deeper resonance in opera than that—curiously he is the subject of all three of the earliest extant operas. That Debussy would even suggest wading back into such a thick history sounds like intellectual bravado—I can only guess he was hoping for some kind of revolution in Segalen's libretto that would at once root and tear away from the cylindrical legend. Not to be; not in his reckoning anyway.

Far more than *In a Sound World*, this is a Symbolist offering—a debt to de Nerval, Bertrand, Mallarmé and Valéry and an exercise in aspects Segalen theorised on in his essay 'Synaesthetics and the Symbolist School'. Gone is the contempt for sight—light, sound and time are now unified into a single force, the resonation of which is too powerful for common man and leaves Orpheus, as the force's lightening rod, so bewildered he cannot tell the present from the future. Further, Orpheus seems to be heavily weighted with a Nietzschean will.

The language has an ebullient plangency to it that is more resounding than anything else Segalen wrote, working to an onomatopoeic echo of the voice and lyre of its subject.

The resultant text is found at times, especially in its stage directions, to be hard to quantify, seemingly describing an emotional rather than a physical environment.

Around 1915 Segalen reworked the 1907-8 drafts which he had set down with Debussy for the libretto into what it is now—ostensibly, a lyric play. It may well have been Debussy's death in 1918 that roused Segalen's determination once more to put *Orphée-Roi* into print, as he must have written the eulogy of dedication to his comrade between then and his own demise the following year. His remarks feel a little febrile in their description and their deference, as if he wrote them whilst in a bit of a state. They end with what seems to attest to his burning of the original manuscript—that joint work, including whatever input Debussy had made. The first publication would appear in 1921 and thus prove posthumous to the both of them.

What answers, what echoes, what revelations lie herein are left to the considerence of your own opinion.

R.W.M.H

Synaesthetics and the Symbolist School

So to the end that goes before we begun—an essay of 1902, five years previous to the publication of *In a Sound World* and seventeen until he'd write the dedication for *Orpheus Rex*.

There are many themes in the works of Segalen, and many works carry little overlap with what lies herein; *Stèles* or his *Voix Mortes*, for instance, swing to a different drum. Yet the present themes creep through the years of his life and make known their reappearances.

These are those that show, despite his searching after a rambling Rimbaud or Gauguin, that, while he can apprehend an overreaching dream, he still knows he'll never leave his own skull; as they did, and, like them, he went anyway.

This final part is a history lesson; a frame frozen; the details preserved are naturally largely forgotten, the depth of thought still interesting. A sapient mind's raillery after a classical education and the sense of something new.

It was quite amazing to find these technical musings that traverse across a story, a myth, a libretto; to apprehend scientific curiosity as artistic output. The permutations are all here.

A conceptual vision of language is drawn up in this essay that was based on what had already been fulfilled and would perhaps reach its apotheosis almost as it was lost—with Apollinaire in the 1st World War, still some way short of the supposed potential that is traced herein.

Segalen vacillates between savouring the endeavours of synaesthetics and an ironic ponderance, (after pondering on those who ironically ponder on it), and it seems to me that in the knowingly-self-congratulatory moment which his character experiences toward the end of *In a Sound World*, after similarly having wavered throughout, he may well have been reflecting on an awareness of this dynamic, present within this earlier essay.

Technically, irony is defined as one thing being used in a manner that is typically antithetical to its perceived intention, so synaesthesia is a fairly natural subject to release an ironic conceit (although strictly, since speaking of synaesthesia is to explicitly refer to a perception that is expected, if not intended, to run opposed to the common understanding of sense, to be ironic would require an element whereby the senses surprisingly work in the standard fashion).

Describing synaesthesia can take some linguistic leaps of imagination, so gird yourself for the ensuing hairpins.

On working through and checking citations I learned a lot about a lot and much of it thankfully. You may find it helpful to keep an encyclopaedia close at hand.

R.W.M.H